Michael Campbell provides th
1919 Bible Conference. Its to
the authority of Ellen G. Wh..
Revelation—continue to be debated and discussed in Adventist circles to this day. To survive and thrive, the Adventism of the future must find the balanced and thoughtful orthodoxy, outlined by Campbell, that Prescott, Daniells, and Willie White were pointing toward during and after the 1919 conference. Until that time, Campbell argues, we will continue to live in the shadows of that defining event.

Nicholas Miller, JD, PhD
Professor of church history
Seventh-day Adventist Theological Seminary
   at Andrews University

Michael Campbell has done a fantastic job and a great service to the Adventist Church by analyzing the historical background that led to the Bible conference in 1919, by describing what transpired during the meetings, and by exploring its impact. In general, Adventists have known very little about the 1919 Bible Conference, organized by the Executive Committee of the General Conference to discuss, among other topics, issues related to prophetic interpretation, the Trinity, and the question of the church's historical transition from having a living prophet among them to having only her writings. Campbell has done the work of a well-trained detective who brings together different pieces of evidence until a picture of what happened is clearly visible. This is a must-read for anyone interested in the way the Lord has been guiding His church and the background of some of the debates that we still observe within the church.

Ángel Manuel Rodríguez, ThD
Former director of the Biblical Research Institute
   of the General Conference

Michael Campbell pulls back the dusty curtain of a seminal event, the 1919 Bible Conference, which sheds light on key theological topics that still occupy our attention today. Through careful research, individuals and issues from one hundred years ago are given much-needed voices that must be heard in the midst of some of our current divisive debates. Fears, anxieties, and strong opinions among these past watchmen on the walls of our faith are permitted to step forward and take center stage among us in Campbell's study and will be also in the minds of the readers who are concerned with current theological trends in the church. Not only does he allow them to be heard, but he uncovers the theological debates of their day, both inside and outside the Seventh-day Adventist Church, that affected their opinions. Hopefully, this book will give us the courage to do the same.

Bill Kilgore, DMin
professor emeritus
Southwestern Adventist University

In this noteworthy book, historian Michael Campbell opens an important window into the turbulent years following Ellen G. White's death when church leaders were struggling to find their theological identity. The forgotten and rediscovered 1919 Bible Conference capitalized on theological and hermeneutical themes that still resonate within the denomination today. Campbell presents, with clarity and efficiency, the historical context of the conference and the major discussions that took place. Each chapter concludes with perspectives and contemporary lessons that speak to all Adventists today, from the pew to the General Conference. This book is a major contribution to Adventist historiography and is ripe with relevance.

Jud Lake, ThD, DMin
Professor of preaching and Adventist studies
Southern Adventist University

For over half a century, few people knew about the discussions that happened at the 1919 Bible Conference, just a few years after Ellen White's death. Church administrators, pastors, and teachers wrestled with obvious challenges to many aspects of Adventist prophetic interpretation and the role the writings of Ellen White should have in biblical and historical interpretations. The opinions were clearly divided, but the shadow of Fundamentalism created a context of hesitation and uncertainty in which honest and candid discussions were impeded and willfully buried. The truth seemed to be inconvenient. Had the transcripts of this conference been made known shortly after it was held, Seventh-day Adventism would likely be vastly different today. Michael Campbell's book re-creates the context, the conversations, and the implications for Adventist history and theology of this forgotten Bible conference. It is a welcome addition to Adventist history, and we should learn from this history as we seek to envision the future of Adventism.

Denis Fortin
Professor of historical theology
Seventh-day Adventist Theological Seminary
   at Andrews University

1919

The Untold Story of Adventism's Struggle With Fundamentalism

The Untold Story of Adventism's Struggle With Fundamentalism

MICHAEL W. CAMPBELL

Nampa, Idaho | www.pacificpress.com

Cover design by Gerald Lee Monks
Cover design photo provided by the author
Inside design by Aaron Troia

Copyright © 2019 by Pacific Press® Publishing Association
Printed in the United States of America
All rights reserved

The author assumes full responsibility for the accuracy of all facts and quotations as cited in this book.

You can obtain additional copies of this book by calling toll-free 1-800-765-6955 or by visiting AdventistBookCenter.com.

Library of Congress Cataloging-in-Publication Data

Names: Campbell, Michael W. (Teacher of Systematic Theology), author.
Title: 1919 : the untold story of Adventism's struggle with fundamentalism / Michael W. Campbell.
Other titles: Nineteen-nineteen
Description: Nampa : Pacific Press Publishing Association, 2019.
Identifiers: LCCN 2019007015 | ISBN 9780816365326 (pbk. : alk. paper)
Subjects: LCSH: General Conference of Seventh-Day Adventists—History. | Seventh-day Adventists—History. | Fundamentalism—History.
Classification: LCC BX6153 .C36 2019 | DDC 286.709—dc23 LC record available at https://lccn.loc.gov/2019007015

March 2019

Dedicated to Heidi

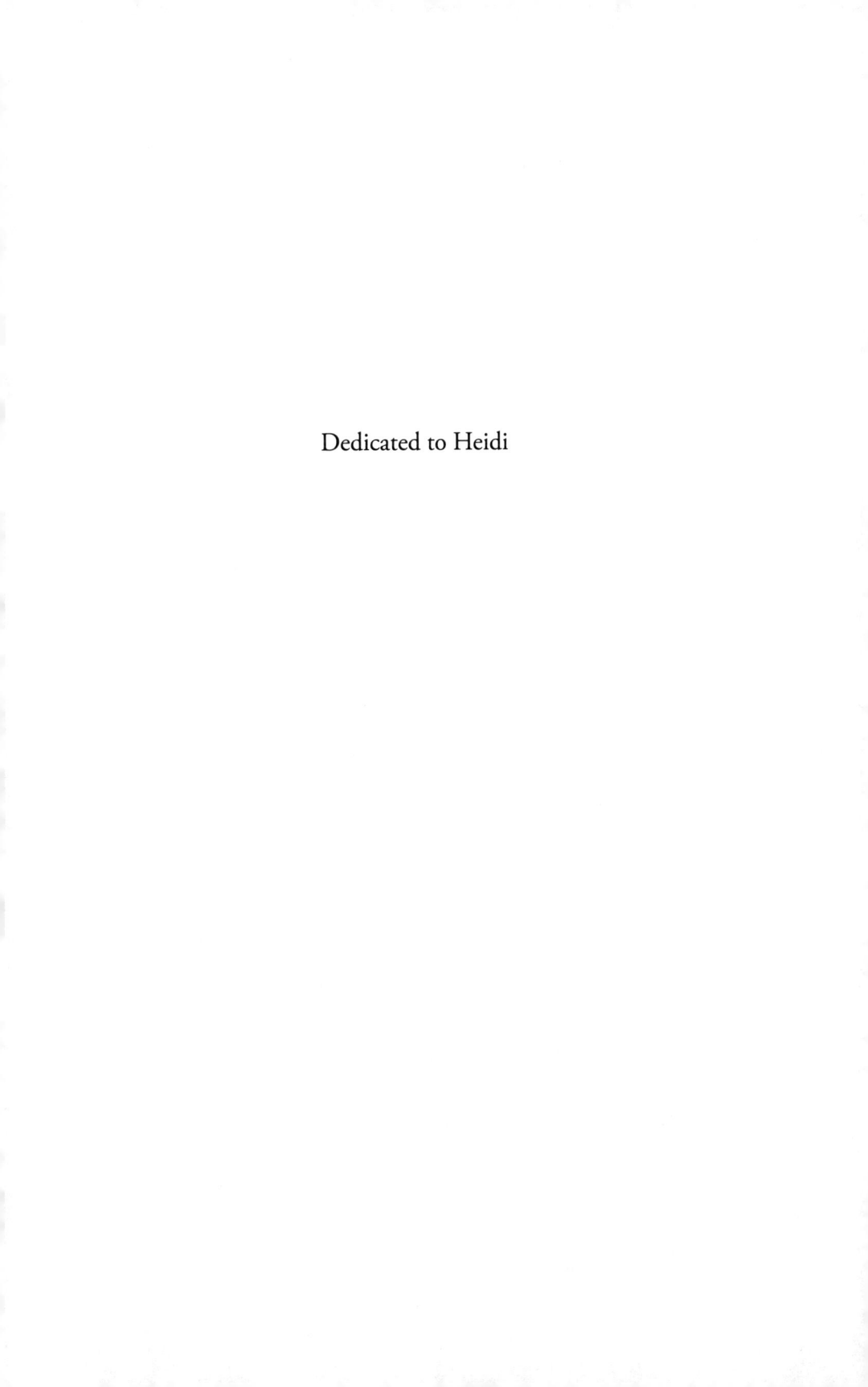

Contents

Foreword 13
Introduction 17

Part 1: Setting the Stage
Chapter 1   Fundamentalist Fling   25
Chapter 2   Without a Living Prophet   37
Chapter 3   The Conference   43
Chapter 4   Adventist Hermeneutics   51

Part 2: Major Issues
Chapter 5   Prophetic Interpretation   63
Chapter 6   The Trinity   73
Chapter 7   Interpreting Ellen White   79
Chapter 8   Teaching History and Training Pastors   97

Part 3: Postlude
Chapter 9   Aftermath   107
Chapter 10 Legacy   113

Foreword

The history of Seventh-day Adventism is marked by a number of notable dates—such as 1844, 1888, 1901, and 1915, just to name a few of the most recognizable. But 1919 had not been on our "screen" of consciousness as an Adventist "household" date before the early 1970s. During these years, Elder Donald Yost located in the newly formed General Conference archives at Takoma Park, Maryland, the "transcripts" recorded at a then relatively little-known conference of church administrators, ministers, and scholars held in 1919. A good sampling of these transcripts was released by Adventist ethicist and editor Roy Branson, who published excerpts of them in *Spectrum*, a journal of opinion, news, and commentary published by the Association of Adventist Forums, a liberal-leaning Adventist group. The release of these transcripts sparked considerable debate regarding a number of theological issues having to do especially with questions related to the doctrine of revelation and the inspiration of the Bible and the writings of Ellen G. White. This event sparked a vigorous debate about the prophetic inspiration and authority of Ellen White and how to best interpret her writings.

The 1919 conference took place in Washington, DC, soon after the end of World War I. This moment in time witnessed the stringent questioning of much "progressive," "liberal"—that is, modernistic—optimism about the perfecting of humanity and their institutions of political, educational, ethical, and cultural uplift in the world. The "Great War" (a common reference to World War I) had effectively brought about a lengthy moment of reflective pause on the part of many thinking people. This helped to open the way for the rise of Evangelical Fundamentalism and its rationalistic burdens about the inerrancy of special revelation.

It is in this setting that we can be better positioned to assess the Adventist and Evangelical dialogues of the mid-1950s and the release of the controversial Adventist book *Seventh-day Adventists Answer Questions on Doctrine* (1957). These dialogues involved Adventist discussions with conservative, Fundamentalist, Evangelical (mostly Reformed) Protestants. Other factors were related to the fact that a number of these conservative Protestant conferees were "Holiness" Wesleyan Evangelicals, who were more in tune with the Methodist and Wesleyan emphases that were so apparent in Adventism's and Ellen White's emphasis on sanctification. Other factors that were in the mix of all of these issues had to do with Christians and military service as well as prophetic interpretation (many Calvinist Evangelicals were interested in dispensationalist currents of thought). All of these Fundamentalist currents would flow into Adventists' attempts to come to terms with their fellow conservative Protestant brothers and sisters.

But there were two other complicating factors that overshadowed the 1919 Bible Conference—the recent death of Ellen G. White in 1915 and the troubling, problematic claims of one of her aspiring, would-be prophetic successors, the scandalous Margaret Rowen in Southern California. The sobering saga of Margaret Rowen is a riveting story, of which most Adventists are largely ignorant. This aspect of Campbell's work has provided quite an informative update (at least for me).

The subject that should be of the most interest to early twenty-first-century Adventists is the issue dealt with in Campbell's chapter 4, which focuses on how Adventists should interpret the Bible. This subject was probably the most critical fault line at the 1919 Bible

Conference between the rising Adventist "progressive" thinkers and the more conservative hard-liners.

So here you have it: a relatively brief book that is chock full of interesting, readable history and theological analysis that together provide a variety of informative insights that should prove helpful to all manner of current Seventh-day Adventist thinkers and students. I know that any attentive reader will come away from the perusal of this compact volume with a much more informed perspective. Such insights will then hopefully enable the reader to be better equipped to think more insightfully about the issues of biblical inspiration and prophecy, varied key aspects of conservative Protestant theology, and the work of self-proclaimed, postcanonical prophetic figures.

Woodrow W. Whidden II
Berrien Springs, Michigan
January 31, 2019

Introduction

After a century it is difficult to find a topic more relevant to Adventism today than the events surrounding the 1919 Bible Conference. This meeting was an epochal event in Seventh-day Adventist history, yet ironically, those who participated could have scarcely realized that they were making history. Only with the passing of time, after the transcripts were discovered in the 1970s, would the theological significance of these discussions become apparent—especially the fact that they were the first major discussion of Ellen White's prophetic authority and how to properly interpret her writings (that is to say, hermeneutics) to take place after her death just four years earlier. At the 1919 Bible Conference, Adventism would find itself polarized across its theological landscape. While the issues raised were not new, the way the participants disagreed with one another was. What had changed? The historical rise of the Fundamentalist movement. A significant part of this book is about both hermeneutics and Adventism's dangerous flirtation with Fundamentalism. Following this conference, the contours of Adventism would forever be changed, and this book further explores the ways in which the denomination was affected by this wider Fundamentalist movement—aspects of which have not been widely known until now.

A word about definitions is imperative before beginning. The terms *Fundamentalism* and *Fundamentalist* are broad, generic terms, used across religions, and often imply some kind of "strict, literal interpretation of scripture" or some kind of conservative adherence to a movement. Such Fundamentalist responses can certainly be found across the centuries and cultures. The historical Fundamentalist Movement, when defined as a reaction to modernism, can be dated with some precision within the American religious landscape. It should be noted that Fundamentalists embrace the same modernist intellectual assumptions that they strived so hard to reject. The publication of three million copies of twelve small, matching books titled *The Fundamentals* (offered free of charge), though not originating the movement, were a catalyst in propelling the movement into widespread public consciousness, even though it would not be until 1922 that Curtis Lee Laws first coined the specific term *Fundamentalist*.

Historian George M. Marsden once quipped that a Fundamentalist was "an Evangelical who is angry about something." Though there was more to it than this, in a sense, he was correct, because the motivation behind the twelve volumes was a perception that the Christian faith was under attack. Many Christians felt the best way to respond to such an attack was to withstand and oppose it. Furthermore, American Christians were traumatized, and even militarized, in the wake of World War I, which put an end to the modernist optimism that humanity could somehow save itself.

Another important term to clarify is *Evangelical*, which for the purpose of this book simply means a Bible-believing Christian who holds a high view of Scripture (that the Bible is truly God's inspired Word) and that the gospel message of the efficacy of Christ's atoning death on the cross must be promulgated to the world. In a very broad sense, an Evangelical is someone who is an heir to the Protestant Reformation, and when defined in this way, Seventh-day Adventists are truly Evangelical Christians. Some Adventists will recall the intense drama surrounding the publication of *Seventh-day Adventists Answer Questions on Doctrine* in 1957. This book came on the heels of dialogue during the 1950s between denominational leaders and certain

Evangelical Christians—who really should be considered Fundamentalists. The 1950s were a formative period, as Billy Graham led those more moderate Fundamentalists to create the American Evangelical Movement. It is important to note that, at the time of the 1919 Bible Conference, this saga was still several decades in the future. I do not believe it is possible to fully realize the scope of these later events without first understanding what happened several decades earlier, in 1919. Both were dramatic episodes in the Adventist hermeneutical landscape. For now, let it suffice to say that the 1919 Bible Conference set the stage for every subsequent hermeneutical battle in Adventist history. Thus, it is essential to understand what happened in 1919 and to do so on its own terms.

A word is in order about how I became interested in this topic. I converted to Adventism at the age of eight with my mother. I gave my first Bible study to my mother, who for a time had stopped attending Bible studies with a small group of ladies that included an Adventist woman and her husband, who happened to be the conference evangelist. Later, as I discovered the story of our Adventist message, I knew two things: I wanted to serve the Lord as a minister of the gospel, and if possible, I would very much like to teach Adventist history. This interest was nurtured as a young person during six summers in which I interned at the Ellen G. White Estate.

By the time I reached college, I had the good fortune to study under the late Benjamin McArthur at Southern Adventist University. One day for class, he assigned us a reading of the final transcripts of the 1919 Bible Conference, which for me, served as a startling revelation that there was a great deal more to how people interpret Ellen White's writings than I had ever realized before. Senior history majors in the class on research methods were assigned a topic on the American Civil War for their senior thesis. But this year, Dr. McArthur told me he wanted me to research the 1919 Bible Conference instead. He did not know that he was sending me on a much larger quest than I could have possibly imagined. Later, as I pursued my graduate studies, I would find myself returning to this topic once again for my dissertation. After more than a decade, I find myself returning to it yet again. While teaching at the Adventist International Institute of Advanced Studies (AIIAS), I taught several courses that reignited the old flame. In particular, I would like to thank students in my last doctoral seminar on Fundamentalism in which they vigorously discussed the latest literature in the field and its relevance for Adventism. Such discussions were a catalyst for the present book. They were also an opportunity to update my research, incorporate into it the latest findings of the past decade, and to recast it in this more popular format for thoughtful Adventists to wrestle with on the anniversary of this epochal event.

A book such as this does not come about by happenstance, and no man is an island. I am grateful to many individuals for their friendship and support and for the various ways in which they have strengthened this book, even though the ultimate responsibility remains with me alone. I would first like to thank the administration of AIIAS as well as my colleagues there, who encouraged me while I wrestled with this topic.

In particular, I want to thank those students in that memorable seminar on Fundamentalism: Adrian Petre, Lowel J. Domocmat, Faith Bayona, and Gabriel Masfa. Each week we would dissect a book and discuss its implications for Adventism. I am also grateful to our library staff at the Leslie Hardinge Library at AIIAS, with particular gratitude to the library director, Megumi Flores. I am furthermore indebted to George R. Knight, Edward Allen, Kevin Burton, and Woodrow Whidden II for their constructive feedback on the manuscript. Special thanks are due also to Jud Lake and Bill Kilgore for their encouragement along the way. A special word of thanks is due to my friend Brian E. Strayer who meticulously read through the manuscript. I'm furthermore grateful to Daniela Pusic, a senior religion major at Southwestern Adventist University with a promising future in academia, who carefully read the manuscript. A debt of gratitude is due to Scott Cady and Miguel Valdivia who guided this book through the editorial process at Pacific Press. I would also like to express appreciation to Eriks Galenieks, who invited me to participate in a forum on the Trinity at the Adventist University of

Africa. Chapter 6 of this book was originally presented as a paper at that conference, was published in their proceedings, and is used in its present form (with some changes) with their permission. I would also like to express appreciation to my colleagues and the administration at Southwestern Adventist University, where we have made our new home this past year.

I am furthermore grateful for such a supportive environment in which to pursue a life of teaching and scholarship. Without such support, this book could not have been written in the midst of an international move and the many aspects of reverse culture shock that happen after spending more than five years of missionary service in the Philippines. Such a global perspective has certainly shaped my outlook in profound ways, and I hope it has enriched this book because we live in an increasingly global Seventh-day Adventist Church, where the majority of our membership now live in what is termed "the Global South." Such considerations are merely the latest aspect of a wider hermeneutical struggle that began in 1919.

Part 1

Setting the Stage

Chapter 1

Fundamentalist Fling

Life in 1919 was anything but certain. Today, after a century, it is difficult to imagine just how different life was for people back then. The world was still reeling after an unprecedented global conflict. World War I left in its wake sixteen million dead. Expectations of human progress lay shattered on the battlefield. Technology that should have facilitated human progress was instead used to kill fellow human beings more effectively and efficiently than ever before in human history. As if this were not enough, a worldwide influenza pandemic wiped out an even more staggering number of people. The most conservative estimates state that globally at least twenty-five million people perished from the disease, and some estimates suggest that number could be quadrupled. So much death only heightened eschatological expectations that the end of the world was nigh.

For many Seventh-day Adventists, such apocalyptic fears confirmed their belief that Jesus was coming again very soon. Adventist evangelists at the time were not shy about getting the word out about what they believed. Yet Adventism was going through an identity crisis of its own. The war raised questions about how church members worldwide should relate to such global catastrophes. As the church grew globally, for the first time it had members on opposite sides of the conflict. This resurrected debates about military service that the church had struggled with at its organization in 1863 when it found itself caught up in the American Civil War.

This chapter provides a contextual background for the rise of Fundamentalism. While the term *Fundamentalism* was initially coined by Curtis Lee Laws in 1922, the movement began much earlier. Two primary catalysts—the rise of the Prophetic Conference Movement and the publication of *The Fundamentals*—were noticed by Seventh-day Adventist thought leaders. It is vital to understand these in order to make sense of the 1919 Bible Conference as well as the relationship of Adventism to Fundamentalism.

The prophetic conference movement

During the opening address of the 1919 Bible Conference, the General Conference president, A. G. Daniells, explained why the church leaders needed to have this meeting. He began with some logistical background (material we will cover in chapter 3) but pointed to a "series of Bible Conferences" organized by Dr. W. B. Riley (1861–1947) as the inspiration for the 1919 meeting. Riley was a rising star in what was known at the time as the Prophetic Conference Movement. The burgeoning conservative Christians making up this movement would come to be known as Fundamentalists. Daniells believed that the work that Riley and others were doing was a model for Adventism. At the outset of the 1919 Bible Conference, he stated that he hoped, this initial meeting following the model of these prophecy conferences, would be the first of a series of annual Bible conferences for Adventists. After all, from his perspective, no meeting like this had ever been held by Adventists before.[1]

Leaders like Riley were harnessing a collective angst within American society caused by the fact that the world they lived in was rapidly changing. In addition to the upheavals of World War I and the influenza pandemic, American culture was rapidly changing in other ways. What was once a predominantly Protestant religious landscape had become a melting pot of religions. The loose nature of the Fundamentalist Movement allowed it to transcend denominational affiliations. The largest number of participants in these prophetic conferences came from either a Presbyterian or Baptist background, yet there were significant numbers from other denominations as well. What united them were four distinct characteristics. First, they cherished their revivalist, evangelical heritage hearkening back to the Protestant Reformation. Second, a renewed interest in endtime events revived a focus on the premillennial return of Christ. Third, many carried some kind of loose affiliation with the Holiness Movement, which arose in the late nineteenth century emphasizing personal piety and holiness in the Christian life. And last, but not least, they embraced militant efforts to defend the faith.[2] These same characteristics would later be echoed within Fundamentalism, and the prophecy conferences were a seedbed from which Fundamentalism arose.

Another rising star in the Prophetic Conference Movement, one whose example would later be referred to by participants at the 1919 Bible Conference, was Arthur T. Pierson (1837–1911). A Presbyterian minister, Pierson rose to prominence for his engagement in world missions. He accepted premillennialism during the summer of 1882 at the Believer's Meeting for Bible Study, which gave further impetus for him to evangelize the world. After Baptist preacher Charles H. Spurgeon passed away, Pierson took the pulpit of the prestigious Metropolitan Tabernacle in London for two years and then returned to teach at Moody Bible Institute. He was a consulting editor for the dispensationalist *Scofield Reference Bible* and later became one of the three primary editors of *The Fundamentals* (more on this later in this chapter). Pierson loomed large on the prophecy conference circuit in the years leading up to and encompassing World War I.

These prophecy conferences were, in reality, a loose network of conservative, evangelical Christians who held to the reliability and inspiration of the Bible. Such conferences renewed their faith in the second coming of Christ as described in the Bible. It would seem that such conservative Christians would resonate closely with Seventh-day Adventists, who also adhered to the soon return of Christ and the authority of Scripture. Instead, these conservative Christians largely ignored the Seventh-day Adventists who attended their meetings.

However, the fact that Adventists were ignored did not lessen the enthusiasm Seventh-day Adventist thought leaders had toward these prophecy conferences. Their admiration resembled a one-sided love affair on the part of Adventist thought leaders. Enthusiasm for these prophecy conferences began with Lee S. Wheeler, an Adventist pastor in Pennsylvania, who was the first to call the church's attention to the prophecy conferences held during World War I. He appreciated their premillennial views and how effectively the meetings garnered public interest in the "subject of Christ's second coming" juxtaposed against the "dark cloud of the present European war." Wheeler traced the origins of the present prophecy conferences to the work of Dwight L. Moody and a significant prophecy conference held in 1878. His initial reporting of these early prophecy conferences certainly caught the eyes of prominent Adventist church leaders.[3]

F. M. Wilcox, the editor of *The Review and Herald*, considered the prophecy conferences to be some of the most significant events in Christian history—parallel to Luther's Ninety-Five Theses and other great religious milestones. Even though Adventists might disagree with their positions on some minor points, these prophecy conferences were significant for Christians, particularly in these last days. The fact that they disagreed on a few matters, such as the seventh-day Sabbath and the state of the dead, was merely evidence that they had not followed through all the way on their convictions about the authority of Scripture and the dangers of modernism. With some input from thoughtful Seventh-day Adventists, Wilcox believed, these spiritual cousins would naturally, over time, become Seventh-day Adventists.

Clearly, Wilcox felt at home at these meetings. In a strange irony of history, Wilcox, one of the more conservative and stalwart Seventh-day Adventist leaders within the denomination at the time, espoused an ecumenical form of Adventism because he resonated strongly with facing a common foe and emphasizing points Adventists held in common with these conservative Christians, who were the harbingers of the rising Fundamentalist movement. Above all, Wilcox admired how successful they were in calling the attention of the world to the soon return of Jesus Christ.

Another influential Adventist of the time was Carlyle B. Haynes. He attended the 1918 Philadelphia Prophecy Conference and reported on his visit in *Signs of the Times*. Haynes believed the meeting was significant because it was drawing attention to the second coming of Christ, a doctrine that he viewed as having lost its emphasis among Protestants. He noted some minor differences between various speakers, yet overall, he appreciated the general tenor of what they were trying to do.

One of the largest prophecy conferences was held November 25–28, 1918, in New York City. This time, Wilcox could not attend, so he sent a *Review and Herald* associate editor, Leon L. Caviness. Caviness was apparently accompanied by Charles T. Emerson, an Adventist evangelist from New England, and possibly a few other individuals. Regarding their experience, Caviness and Emerson shared: "The keynote of the first meeting, as well as of the whole conference, and the point emphasized by every speaker, was the personal, literal, imminent, premillennial coming of the Lord Jesus Christ." Such widespread interest in this conference, Caviness believed, would open doors for Adventists to share their faith. He saw his visit as an opening of his eyes similar to the experience of Elijah, who discovered that there were many more who had "not bowed the knee to Baal."[4] Of special interest for Caviness were the presentations at this prophecy conference about the infallibility of the Bible. Clearly, this meeting "was one of the most successful religious gatherings ever held in this city [New York] in recent years."[5] He was nothing short of enthusiastic about how many there were who shared his faith in the soon return of Jesus Christ, and who affirmed the authority of Scripture in contrast to the speculative winds of doctrine that would shake the confidence of people in the divine inspiration of God's Word.

The nascent Fundamentalists holding these conferences just before and during World War I were part of a group of conservative Christians who after the war and through the 1920s would coalesce into a much more clearly defined, and militant, historical movement.

As various Seventh-day Adventists attended these prophetic conferences, they clearly admired the work that these people were doing in calling the attention of the world to the soon return of Jesus Christ. As a consequence, these Adventist thought leaders clearly saw the conferences as having great historical significance and believed they were aligned with Adventists in warning the world about Christ's return. While they recognized there were some minor differences between Adventist beliefs and those of the speakers at these conferences, they also knew that there were some differences among the various speakers themselves at these meetings about how the end would take place. What united them was the fact that they shared common enemies in those who sought to undermine the authority of Scripture.

Although Adventists who attended these meetings were excited about the publicity being given to the Second Advent, it appears that theirs was a one-sided love affair. No Adventist was ever asked to speak at these meetings, and although the extant records acknowledge a wide variety of persons from different faiths as having participated, no mention was ever made of any Adventist participants.

The Fundamentals

In addition to these prophecy conferences, another major catalyst behind what eventually became the historic Fundamentalist movement was a series of pamphlets titled, simply, *The Fundamentals: A Testimony to the Truth*. Their original purpose was quite simple. The goal was to widely disseminate conservative Christian values and beliefs in a culture that no longer placed authority in the divine inspiration of Scripture.

The publication of these pamphlets was innocuous enough. Two oil tycoons in the Standard Oil Company, Lyman and Milton Stewart, had used their fortune to fund a wide variety of philanthropic projects, ranging from overseas missions to the education of Bible college teachers. In 1908, Lyman Stewart devoted a large portion of his estate to develop the Bible Institute of Los Angeles (BIOLA), after which he gave only token financial gifts to other worthwhile endeavors.

The initial impetus behind founding BIOLA, according to Lyman Stewart, was to create a theological safe haven where the authority of God's Word would never be questioned. He was especially concerned when he discovered that, during the 1890s, a teacher at Occidental College had questioned supernatural aspects of the biblical narrative—in spite of the fact that Stewart had funded not only that teacher's position but the entire Bible department! This teacher's use of historical-critical methods was considered "positively devilish" because it destroyed faith in the "absolute inerrancy" of Scripture. In order to make sure his funds were never again diverted to such nefarious schemes, Stewart envisioned a modest Bible school under his guidance.[6]

Stewart also had a much wider vision of warning Christians everywhere against liberal Bible teachers who, from his perspective, undermined the reliability of Scripture. He envisioned publishing Christian literature that would refute modernist authors who undermined the Word of God. This publishing effort would become the largest recipient of his funds outside of the Bible Institute of Los Angeles. Stewart recruited A. C. Dixon, pastor of the Moody Church in Chicago, to head this project. He suggested that Dixon contact potential authors to produce a "series of articles" to warn "all the Anglo-Saxon Protestant ministers, missionaries and theological students in the world."[7] After 1913, Dixon was succeeded by R. A. Torrey, and then by Louis Meyer. Yet the purpose of the project always remained the same. Christians must be warned about any dangerous forms of liberal Christianity that might undermine the supernatural claims found in the Bible. By 1914 and the beginning of World War I, the Stewart brothers had financed the circulation of over three million copies of *The Fundamentals* at the cost of $200,000. Thus, this publication gave the Fundamentalist movement its enduring name.[8]

The booklets contained ninety articles from sixty-four different authors. These contributors included "a broad range of conservative and millenarian scholars, ministers, and laypersons"[9] from America, Britain, and Canada. *The Fundamentals* addressed three main themes. Approximately one-third of the articles dealt with the inspiration of Scripture and generally endorsed a view of infallibility and verbal inerrancy, at least of the original autographs. (This view stood in contrast to Ellen White's endorsement of thought inspiration as opposed to verbal dictation.) Another third dealt with traditional theological pillars, including the Trinity, sin, and salvation. The last third of the articles contained personal testimonies, attacks against competing, aberrant forms of Christianity (such as Mormonism and Roman Catholicism), the relationship between science and religion, and general appeals for support of missions and evangelism. Altogether, these articles show that although the emerging Fundamentalist movement did not have a clearly defined set of beliefs, its adherents knew what it was against: anyone and anything that might challenge the divine authority of Scripture.

It is difficult to assess the impact of *The Fundamentals*. One historian, Ernest R. Sandeen, argues that these booklets had "little impact upon biblical studies."[10] Despite the media blitz, it seems that the average Christian layperson still remained largely unaware of historical criticism of the Bible, which remained primarily in the purview of scholars, or at least of those who paid attention to scholarly works. Yet for Fundamentalists, such concerns became "the origin of their crusade."[11] For some lay people, *The Fundamentals* sensitized them that such debates about the critical study of the Bible existed. Furthermore, these publications helped coalesce such concerns into an emerging movement.

In the same way that Seventh-day Adventists noticed, and even attended, the prophetic conferences, Adventist thought leaders also took notice of the publication of *The Fundamentals*. One of the first persons to notice these publications was Stephen N. Haskell, a veteran Adventist minister, who had become embattled in several controversies within the Seventh-day Adventist Church during the early twentieth century. Haskell viewed himself as a stalwart defender of the prophetic writings of Ellen G. White, even going so far as to argue that they were an infallible lens for interpreting the Bible and that her writings were infallible and inerrant.

Thus, Haskell grew concerned when some people tampered with, or revised her writings. Of special concern to him were those historians who proposed changes to the 1911 edition of Ellen G. White's *The Great Controversy*, the story of church history from the close of the apostolic era through end-time events. Haskell resonated with articles in *The Fundamentals* regarding inerrancy that he saw as being in harmony with his own views of inspiration.[12]

By and large, however *The Fundamentals* did not receive widespread attention within Seventh-day Adventism. W. W. Prescott, one of the most visible persons at the 1919 Bible Conference, referenced these booklets in the published version of his presentations. Some church periodicals also carried advertisements for *The Fundamentals*. Within Adventism, at least for those who were paying attention, this was a wake-up call that times were changing. Adventists in general resonated with the same kinds of concerns that they saw published in *The Fundamentals*.[13]

Uncertain times

In addition to the prophetic conferences and the publication of *The Fundamentals*, there was much evidence that life was uncertain in the 1910s. Most significant of all was World War I, the dominant event of this time period, although it did not directly affect the United States until 1917. But once America was in the war, Adventists were affected in several important ways. Evangelists cited the conflict as proof of Christ's impending return, but the war also had an impact on the church in more tangible ways. Church leaders were once again confronted with the problem of military service. Overseas missionaries were cut off as communication and even finances slowed to a trickle or even ceased completely at times. Tragically, English missionary Homer R. Salisbury perished when the ship he was sailing on was sunk by a submarine in the Mediterranean Sea.[14] Some Adventists brought into question their loyalty to a country—the United States—that was identified eschatologically as the lamblike beast that becomes oppressive as described in Revelation 13. Adventists were cognizant that the end could be near as new discussions about Sunday laws were brought up in some areas.[15]

It is not surprising, therefore, that as tensions about war increased, Adventists saw the emerging conflict as a fulfillment of prophecy. Just how significant this event was considered to be varied among Adventist interpreters. Traditional interpretations, most notably that of Uriah Smith in his landmark book *Thoughts on Daniel and The Revelation,* published and republished in numerous editions from 1865 onward, argued that a final battle would take place between the king of the north (which Smith identified as Turkey) versus the king of the south (identified as Egypt).[16] Smith believed Turkey would be propped up until "he shall come to his end" (Daniel 11:45). This would mark the beginning of Armageddon. Adventist expositors referred to this as the "Eastern Question" in discussions of the fate of the Ottoman Empire, or Turkey. When Turkey suffered defeats in 1912 and 1913 from the armies of the Balkan League, Adventists drew upon Daniel 11 and Revelation 16 to predict that the Turks would be driven from Europe and temporarily relocate to Jerusalem, and then the "great time of trouble" would usher in the end.[17]

Adventists used the uncertainty generated by the war as an opportunity for evangelism. The *Review and Herald* printed a *War Extra* that sold fifty thousand copies per day during its first week of publication, and then followed it with a bonus *Eastern Question Extra*. Both eventually sold well over a million copies. Despite cautions by church leaders in the *Review and Herald* not to sensationalize the war by jumping too quickly to conclusions about the fulfillment of prophecy, many Adventists echoed Percy T. Magan's assertion that the words *Mene, Mene* were "written across the lintel of the Turkish house."[18]

Adventist historian Gary Land, in his analysis of this conflict, concluded that Adventist predictions were supplanted by rapidly changing events; for example, Adventists could not explain the British victory over the Turks at Jerusalem on December 9, 1917. Although Adventists maintained a "general expectation of impending disaster," the fact that so many Adventist expositors had jumped the gun and now were wrong showed that earlier cautions by church leaders were justified. Over the next couple of years, "Adventist interest in Turkey," adds Land, "continued to flicker" as a few diehards still urged that "Turkey's end was very near."[19]

World War I affected Seventh-day Adventists in other ways beyond their interpretation of prophecy. Adventists in Europe were split on the issue of military service. The widespread devastation affected the church broadly as members on both sides of the Atlantic focused their efforts on humanitarian relief. Adventists were encouraged to donate to the American Red Cross, and after the war, denominational relief efforts took more tangible shape, resulting in the Church organizing an Adventist relief agency of its own. Today, the organization is known as the Adventist Development and Relief Agency.

Perspective
Some Seventh-day Adventists during the time just before and during World War I (1914–1918) were flirting with Fundamentalism, including its somewhat rigid views of biblical inspiration. The war heightened eschatological expectations as Adventists saw in it the fulfillment of Bible prophecy. At the same time, they were envious of the success of their conservative Protestant Christians who garnered increasingly large crowds as they called the attention of the public to the soon return of Jesus. Adventist leaders attended these gatherings and reported on them with enthusiasm in church periodicals. They noted minor theological differences, but they downplayed these and emphasized, instead, similarities and the significance of these events for Christian history. Likewise, although not quite so effusively, Adventist thought leaders noticed, and promoted, the publication of *The Fundamentals*—the main catalyst behind these publications' namesake movement. The concerns of the Fundamentalists resonated with Adventists, at least those who paid attention to what was going on around them as society changed and new, liberal forms of modernist Christianity invaded the classroom.

1. Report of Bible Conference, July 1, 1919, 11, 12.
2. Donald W. Dayton, "Introduction," in *The Prophecy Conference Movement*, ed. Donald W. Dayton, vol. 1, *Fundamentalism in American Religion, 1880–1950* (New York: Garland, 1988).
3. Lee S. Wheeler, "A Deepening Conviction: Prominent Men of Many Persuasions Earnestly Proclaim the Doctrine—The Events of the Time Compel Serious Reflection," *Signs of the Times*, June 1, 1915, 337, 338.
4. Leon L. Caviness, "The Prophetic Conference, New York City," *Review and Herald*, December 12, 1918, 1, 2.
5. Charles T. Emerson, "The Prophetic Conference," *The Watchman Magazine*, March 23, 1919, 29–30.
6. For background on this discussion, see Lyman Stewart to L. H. Severance, June 8, 1909, BIOLA University Archives and Special Collections, Letter notebook #1, 121–123.
7. Lyman Stewart to Charles C. Cook, February 28, 1910, BIOLA University Archives and Special Collecitons, Letter notebook #3, 127.
8. For an overview of this, see George M. Marsden, *Fundamentalism and American Culture*, 2nd ed. (New York: Oxford University Press, 2006), 119.
9. Marsden, *Fundamentalism and American Culture*, 119.
10. Ernest R. Sandeen, *The Roots of Fundamentalism: British and American Millenarianism 1800–1930* (Chicago: University of Chicago Press, 1970), 188–207.
11. Marsden, *Fundamentalism and American Culture*, 118–123.
12. For a discussion of Haskell and his view of inspiration, see Denis Kaiser, "Trust and Doubt: Perceptions of Divine Inspiration in Seventh-day Adventist History (1880–1930)" (PhD diss., Andrews University, 2016), 301–323.
13. See Kaiser, "Trust and Doubt," 310–312.
14. For details on the story, see Koberson Langhu, "The Origin and Development of the Seventh-day Adventist Church in India (1895–1947)" (PhD diss., Adventist International Institute of Advanced Studies, 2017), 155, 156.
15. For a discussion, see Michael W. Campbell, "The 1919 Bible Conference and Its Significance for Seventh-day Adventist History and Theology" (PhD diss., Andrews University, 2008), 23, 24.
16. See Uriah Smith, *Daniel and The Revelation* (Battle Creek, MI: Review and Herald®, 1897), 203–318.
17. For a helpful background, see Gary Land, "The Perils of Prophecying: Seventh-day Adventists Interpret World War One," *Adventist Heritage* 1, no. 1 (January 1974): 28–33, 55, 56.
18. Percy T. Magan, *The Vatican and the War; A Retrospect and Forecast: Being a Review of the Past Attitudes of the Vatican Towards Civil and Religious Government, and an Analysis of Her Latest Utterances Upon These Matters as Related to the European War* (Nashville, TN: Southern Publishing Association, 1915); See also, F. M. Wilcox, "A Time to Pray," *Review and Herald*, August 13, 1914, 6.
19. Land, "Seventh-day Adventists Interpret World War One," 33, 55, 56.

CHAPTER 2

Without a Living Prophet

An issue even more critical to Adventism's identity was the fact that the last of the denomination's early pioneers were fast disappearing from the scene of action. The Adventist prophetess Ellen G. White, whose counsel had guided the fledgling denomination through its infancy and adolescence, died in 1915. Would there be another prophetic successor? How would the denomination treat Mrs. White's writings without her living, prophetic voice? These questions weighed heavily on the minds of church members a century ago.

The death of Ellen G. White
By 1910 Ellen White was eighty-two years old and recognized her own impending mortality. As a leader of the Seventh-day Adventist Church for over six decades, she recognized that her writings would be a permanent legacy that would continue to testify until the eschaton.[1] Her driving passion during the last years of her life was the translation and publication of her writings. Some of the most significant of these during her final years included *The Acts of the Apostles* (1911), and an updated edition of her classic work on Christian history and end-time events, *The Great Controversy* (1911).

She had trusted literary assistants to do historical research that helped her complete these and other volumes. She also began to assemble a new edition of her autobiography, *Life Sketches*, which came out posthumously, with the last section written by her stalwart assistant, C. C. Crisler. Thus the publication of her final writings, as well as the planning, disposition, and control of her literary estate were matters of great importance to Ellen White as she embraced her own mortality.

In order to facilitate this process, she prepared in 1912 the final version of her last will and testament. It created a self-perpetuating board of five trustees who would control her literary estate. One-fourth of her estate was left for family, with the remainder given to the church she loved so much.

A portent of the end came on February 15, 1915, when Ellen White fell in her home. Over the next five months, regular updates about her health appeared in the *Review and Herald* until her death on July 16, 1915.[2] In anticipation of her death, church leaders had prepared a press release with pictures for newspapers across the country. A series of three funerals was held. The first took place on the lawn of "Elmshaven," her home in Saint Helena, California. A second was held at a camp meeting in the San Francisco Bay area. A third and final service was conducted in the Battle Creek Tabernacle at Battle Creek, Michigan, where she was interred in nearby Oak Hill Cemetery next to her husband and other loved ones. Thousands came to these funerals to show their respect. The denomination honored her through many tributes published in church periodicals.

In many ways, Adventists after her death continued to function as if they still had a living prophet. Articles were reprinted or gleaned from her unpublished writings as if she were still alive. One final book manuscript appeared about Old Testament history, *Prophets and Kings*, whose last two chapters of which were pieced together from previously unpublished articles and manuscripts. This completed the five-volume Conflict of the Ages series spanning the cosmic controversy between Christ and Satan from the birth of sin until its final eradication at the last judgment.[3]

It would not be until the 1919 Bible Conference that Adventist thought leaders seriously wrestled with what it meant to no longer have a living prophetic voice. There were significant ramifications for how the denomination would view her writings. As a consequence, the reality of living without a living prophet loomed large in Adventist minds at this time.

Margaret Rowen

If the reality of being without a living prophet were not enough, the situation also raised questions about the possibility of a prophetic successor. Hardly had Ellen White's body become cold in the grave when a self-proclaimed successor sought her prophetic mantle. On June 22, 1916, less than a year after Ellen White's death, a recent convert from Methodism, Margaret Rowen, supposedly received visionary manifestations. One such report described this thirty-five-year-old woman as holding her hands "folded across her breast . . . [her] wide-open, unwinking eyes looking upward. . . . There was no breathing, as far as we could tell, and the body was rigid."[4] Had God in fact transferred the prophetic mantle? The lack of a living prophet meant that Ellen White was no longer available to distinguish between herself and imposters.

Church leaders from both the Southern California Conference and the Pacific Union Conference urged members to exercise caution "before expressing judgment in the matter." Some of Rowen's earliest visions were published in a booklet, *A Stirring Message for This Time*. Contemporary Adventists would likely have noticed some theological red flags: seven years between each of the seven last plagues, the judgment throne enclosed in a temple of silver, and a "great and terrible storm" that was to occur right after the close of probation. Despite these anomalies, Rowen's visions did appear remarkably similar to the scenario of end-time events described by Ellen White in *The Great Controversy*. By the time of the 1919 Bible Conference, her prophetic claims would have been on the minds of conference participants.

In fact, after the Bible conference, in the autumn of 1919, Margaret Rowen made the sensational claim that in the manuscript files of the White Estate was a letter, dated August 10, 1911, in Saint

Helena, California, in which Ellen White had stated that Rowen would be a future messenger of God.

When W. C. White, son of Ellen White and secretary of the White Estate Board, looked through the manuscript files, he found the document, much to his chagrin. However, it bore immediate evidence of a forgery—the sheets were not perforated like other documents in the file, the typeface was different, there was no document file number, Ellen White had not been in Saint Helena on the date of the document, and the signature was a demonstrable forgery. The question lingered: How could this document have gotten into the White Estate files?

Yet Rowen gradually developed a small but loyal group of followers who claimed that she was a divinely sent messenger. Her local congregation, however, was apparently not convinced by her claims. She was disfellowshiped from the South Side Seventh-day Adventist Church in Los Angeles on November 15, 1919. With a spiritual martyr as their leader, her followers organized themselves into a new denomination, taking the name The Los Angeles, California, Seventh-day Adventist Reform Church, pejoratively referred to as "Rowenites."

As an official organization, Rowen's Reform Church accepted tithe funds. Questions arose about her family background, causing her to make unusual claims in order to justify her prophetic calling. By November 1923, Rowen announced that the close of probation would occur on February 6, 1924, and that Christ would come in glory on February 6, 1925. Such a sensational announcement received widespread media attention that brought embarrassment to Seventh-day Adventists. When the prediction failed, her band of followers began to disintegrate.

One of Margaret Rowen's earliest supporters and largest financial backers was a Burt B. Fullmer, a physician in the Los Angeles area. Shortly after the failure of the predicted time for the Lord's return, Fullmer discovered that Rowen had been stealing from her own organization. Disenchanted with the lack of integrity manifested by such actions, he confessed on March 12, 1926, to inserting the spurious letter naming Rowen as Ellen White's successor into an open drawer in the White Estate vault.

It was a time when physicians made house calls, and late one night Dr. Fullmer received a call to a nearby motel. As he entered the room, he was struck on the head by a piece of pipe. Motel guests who heard the commotion summoned the police. When they arrived on the scene, they found Rowen and two co-conspirators with a shovel, a burlap sack, and rope. The three fled but were quickly apprehended.

Once again, Rowen found herself at the center of a media storm as newspapers covered the trial. All three were sentenced to prison terms for "assault with a deadly weapon, with intent to do great bodily harm." Dr. Fullmer, however, died before the court proceeded with sentencing. About a year later, Rowen was released from prison, fled parole, and disappeared from public life. Recent research suggests that she moved to Florida under a pseudonym. She is believed to have died in the early 1950s.

This bizarre story reveals in part how Adventists, after the death of Ellen White, were struggling with how to deal with the fact that they no longer had a living prophetic voice. Would God bestow the mantle on a successor? Questions like this loomed large in the minds of Adventists during the time period leading up to the 1919 Bible Conference. As the saying goes, truth is stranger than fiction. Entangled in a web of lies, Rowen found herself having to make increasingly dramatic claims until she eventually predicted the end of the world. Many Adventists who wanted so badly to believe her claims were willing to overlook inconsistencies in the life of this charismatic "almost prophetess."

Prophetic perspective

As the early pioneers quietly passed away, no death was more traumatic than that of the Adventist prophetess, Ellen G. White. Her death meant that, for the first time, the denomination had to grapple with life without a living prophet. At first, like an individual going through the stages of grief, Adventism seemed as if it were in denial; the church continued to function as if Ellen White were still around.

It simply kept republishing articles or creating new ones out of unpublished manuscripts. As time went on, this created a lacuna that individuals such as Margaret Rowen tried to exploit by claiming to be Ellen White's prophetic successors. Rowen's saga, one of the most bizarre tales from our Adventist past, and similar claims by others launched the church into a decade-long controversy about the legitimacy of Ellen White's prophetic mantle. Over time, this issue became increasingly problematic and was quickly repudiated. Yet in 1919 none of this was at all certain, and Margaret Rowen still loomed on the horizon as church leaders wrestled with her claims. One thing was clear—denominational leaders needed to discuss what, exactly, was the significance of White's writings and how those writings should be interpreted. Thus, hermeneutics (the way that inspired writings are interpreted) would become a central focus of the 1919 Bible Conference. And while the interpretation and authority of Ellen White's writings were not initially included on the agenda, it should come as no surprise that the issue arose repeatedly throughout the meeting.

---

1. W. C. White, "Confidence in God," *General Conference Bulletin*, June 1, 1913; Ellen G. White, *The Writing and Sending Out of the Testimonies for the Church* (Mountain View, CA: Pacific Press®, 1913), 13, 14.

2. For an overview of these final five months, see Arthur L. White, *Ellen G. White: The Later Elmshaven Years, 1905–1915* (Washington, DC: Review and Herald®, 1982), 418–431; Jerry Moon, *W. C. White and Ellen G. White: The Relationship Between the Prophet and Her Son* (Berrien Springs, MI: Andrews University Press, 1993).

3. See Denis Fortin and Jerry Moon, eds., *The Ellen G. White Encyclopedia* (Hagerstown, MD: Review and Herald®, 2013), s.v. "Conflict of the Ages Series."

4. Fortin and Moon, *Ellen G. White Encyclopedia*, s.v. "Margaret Matilda (Wright) Rowen."

Chapter 3

The Conference

In the second decade of the twentieth century, a variety of concerns converged, causing church leaders to feel that it was imperative for influential thought leaders within the Seventh-day Adventist Church to gather for a Bible conference. Such meetings were not new to Adventism—after all, between 1848 and 1850, the earliest Sabbatarian Adventist pioneers gathered for a series of important Bible conferences to study and pray. Together, they wrestled to discover important biblical truths that became important aspects of Adventist identity. Now, new eschatological expectations, in large part generated by World War I and the death of Ellen White, meant that such a Bible conference would be valuable for the denomination once again.

Seventh-day Adventists love to hold meetings. Beginning with the 1891 Harbor Springs Convention, the denomination periodically gathered educators to discuss educational needs. By 1919, such conferences and conventions had become a common way to deal with theological and pedagogical challenges. In 1919 alone, the Church held seven other major conventions in addition to the 1919 Bible Conference, which is the focus of this book. Other meetings included a convention for secretaries and treasurers, a colporteur convention, an educational convention, an editorial convention, an evangelist convention, a foreign workers convention, and a home missionary (lay evangelism) convention.[1]

It is not surprising, then, that church leaders began to plan for a major Bible conference that would facilitate a "deeper and more cooperative study of the Word of God."[2] Although this 1919 Bible Conference was not the largest, it would be the longest of any of these church gatherings held in 1919 and, with the passing of time, certainly would become the most famous.

Early plans

Even before World War I, there had been rumblings by church leaders for a Bible conference. In 1913, Adventist editor M. C. Wilcox made a private appeal to the General Conference president, A. G. Daniells, to hold such a meeting in order to promote "in-depth Bible study."[3] Unfortunately, such plans did not amount to anything tangible. Then on April 15, 1918, seven months before the end of World War I, the General Conference Executive Committee passed a series of three resolutions. First, it voted to have a "council" that would meet in Washington, DC, for six weeks beginning on July 1 of that year. Second, the delegation to the council was to be "made up of the Bible and History teachers in our colleges and junior colleges, leading editors, and such other leading men as the General Conference Committee may designate; also that our twelve-grade academies be invited to send a delegate of their own selection." And third, the union or local conferences were to cover the transportation costs of delegates with some assistance from the General Conference. The committee also voted to accept the generous offer from the administration of Washington Missionary College (today, Washington Adventist University) to provide free housing for delegates.[4]

As plans for a Bible conference shaped up further, the General Conference Spring Council on April 29 appointed a planning committee consisting of five individuals—W. W. Prescott, M. C. Wilcox, J. L. Shaw, W. E. Howell, and F. M. Wilcox—to lay the groundwork for the upcoming Bible conference. As the time drew near, the committee felt more time was needed, so on May 20, the conference was postponed until July 7, and attendance was limited to Bible and history teachers.[5] Unfortunately, these plans for a Bible conference in 1918 had to be postponed yet again until 1919. On June 5, 1918, Daniells suggested to the General Conference Committee that it delay the Bible conference due to the high cost of travel and travel restrictions related to the war. Thus, the Bible conference was pushed forward to the summer of 1919.[6]

Describing this formative time when the possibility of a Bible conference was initially being discussed, J. L. Shaw, one of the members of the planning committee, observed that some of the committee members "finally got their courage up to the point of recommending the holding of such a conference, for the spiritual uplift of our men, and for the purpose of a [sic] studying together some lines of truth that appear to need united consideration."[7] It is unclear who chaired this early meeting or why they needed to "get their courage up." Perhaps they were afraid to propose a meeting at which varying viewpoints would be presented.

Instead, the official minutes document that a Bible conference should be held "at an early date for prayerful study of the Word." The planning committee would "recommend the date, topics for study, and men to give consideration to topics named." The planning committee remained the same. It seems possible that W. E. Howell may have chaired the early phase of the committee, although Gilbert Valentine argues that W. W. Prescott, one of the most visible persons at the 1919 Bible Conference, ultimately chaired this planning group.[8]

Three days after the formation of the committee, it made the following recommendations:

1. [A] Bible Conference of representative workers be held for a period of three weeks, July 1 to 21.
2. [T]his conference be attended by the following persons:
    a. Such members of the General Conference Committee in the United States and Canada as can arrange to attend.

>   b. Editors: F M Wilcox, A O Tait, A W Spaulding, M C Wilcox, C P Bollman, D E Robinson.
>   c. Teachers: The Bible and History teachers from our colleges, junior colleges, and seminaries.
> 3. [T]he place be left to the General Conference Committee to determine.
> 4. [A]t the conclusion of this conference the Bible and History teachers remain together another three weeks to work on constructive teaching plans. . . .
> 5. [A] committee of seven be appointed by the chair to arrange the program, place, and all details pertaining to the conferences, including expense. Named: W E Howell, F M Wilcox, W W Prescott, A W Spaulding, M C Wilcox, M E Kern, R D Quinn.[9]

The planning committee returned the next day with recommendations. First, that the gathering be held in Petoskey, Michigan, if they could find proper facilities. If this did not work out, they would try next for Denver, Colorado. If neither location worked out, it would be referred back to the General Conference Committee. Second, they would pool expenses and provide seventy-five cents per day for each participant. Third, the topics to be discussed should include "The Person of Christ, The Mediatorial Work of Christ, The Nature and Work of the Holy Spirit, The Two Covenants, The Principles of Prophetic Interpretation, The Eastern Question, The Beast Power in Revelation, The 1260 Days, The United States in Prophecy, The Seven Trumpets, [and] Matthew Twenty-four."[10]

Plans to hold the Bible conference in Michigan or Colorado fell through. The General Conference Committee on May 23, 1919, voted that the attraction of being near major research libraries and archival materials meant that Takoma Park, Washington, DC, the place they had originally planned to hold the conference, would be an ideal location.[11] The only objection to the Washington, DC, location, church leaders noted, was the potential for hot weather. Meetings would be held in the basement of the newly constructed

Columbia Hall at Washington Missionary College to make things more tolerable (in an age before air-conditioning).

Official letters of invitation went out on June 3, 1919. The list of topics now included more specific assignments: (1) the person and mediatorial work of Christ (W. W. Prescott); (2) the nature and work of the Holy Spirit (A. G. Daniells); (3) the two covenants (F. M. Burg); (4) the principles of prophetic interpretation (M. C. Wilcox); (5) the Eastern Question (H. C. Lacey and C. M. Sorenson); (6) the beast power of Revelation (M. C. Wilcox); (7) the 1,260 days (H. S. Prenier); (8) the United States in prophecy (W. H. Wakeham); (9) the seven trumpets (M. L. Andreasen and C. L. Benson); (10) Matthew 24 (W. W. Prescott); and (11) the identification of the ten kingdoms (C. P. Bollman). This list would continue to be refined as the time drew closer. In conclusion, Howell stated that it was the committee's "aim to make the bible [sic] Conference strongly spiritual in every respect."[12] He noted that presentations would be followed by a season of prayer.

The conference
After all of this careful planning, the 1919 Bible Conference finally convened at Washington Missionary College in Takoma Park, Maryland. As previously mentioned, the main meetings were held in the basement of the newly built Columbia Hall to provide a cooler environment, which turned out to be a good thing because that particular summer posted record high temperatures. The building was new, and participants later rejoiced when partway through the Bible conference screens were put up on the windows to block the sweltering sun. The conference began on July 1 and continued through August 9, 1919.[13]

Most of what we know about the 1919 Bible Conference comes from stenographic transcripts of some of the meetings, as well as from published reports in the *Review and Herald* and references in unpublished letters and diaries. While the transcripts are extensive, they are far from exhaustive. When topics became heated, A. G. Daniells at times asked stenographers to stop recording or to strike certain portions of the meeting from the record. The only reason we know this is because the stenographers recorded his request before ceasing their transcription![14]

The Bible conference (July 1–19) was held concurrently with the Bible and History Teachers' Council, which continued for another three weeks until August 9. The Bible conference was held during the early morning and afternoon, thus allowing a break during the hottest part of the day. The teachers usually met during the evening to discuss pedagogical matters. Only 15 percent of the transcripts from the meetings of the Bible and History Teachers' Council are extant, although these include some of the most controversial records as will be discussed later.

When the 1919 Bible Conference actually began, the General Conference president, A. G. Daniells, chaired most of the meetings. W. E. Howell, secretary of the Education Department, served as conference secretary and also chaired the Bible and History Teachers' Council. F. M. Wilcox served as chair of an "Editorial Committee." C. M. Sorenson and E. F. Albertsworth served as official "librarians" for the conference—presumably to help participants find research materials and to take advantage of the many resources available in the area. S. M. Butler chaired the "Entertainment Committee," which supervised the housing and feeding of delegates.

The purpose of the 1919 Bible Conference was to study the "various phases of our truth." Daniells noted that there was some fear of getting into unhelpful controversy, but he emphasized how much more important it was for those gathered to enter into a deeper and more cooperative study of God's Word. They could give "careful study to the majoy [sic] questions, the great essentials, the fundamentals." Daniells hoped that the 1919 Bible Conference would lead to greater unity among leading thinkers in the denomination.[15]

A total of sixty-five individuals are known to have participated in the 1919 Bible Conference.[16] Of these, twenty-nine were educators from fourteen different schools; eleven were editors; and twenty-five were church administrators or support staff. A total of three women were present, and the average age of participants was forty-five.

These sixty-five individuals represented the best-trained group of Adventist thought leaders to ever gather up until that time. Whereas prior gatherings certainly were composed of very competent individuals, this gathering was particularly notable for the number of participants who were fluent in biblical languages. During discussions at the 1919 Bible Conference, participants could go into great depth about the etymology of a word or the syntax of a phrase from Scripture. Participants utilized many different Bible translations and referenced some of the best scholarly resources, including various historical, biblical, and other academic literature. Some conferees had advanced training in historical methods and used scholarly resources available in French and German. The first two Seventh-day Adventists to earn PhDs were present at this meeting. B. G. Wilkinson and E. F. Albertsworth had earned doctorates from George Washington University in 1908 and 1918, respectively. In a sense, the 1919 Bible Conference could be considered the first "scholarly" gathering in Seventh-day Adventist history.

Despite all the careful planning, the topic that ultimately dominated the 1919 Bible Conference was that of hermeneutics, or how to properly interpret inspired writings. Chapter 4 of this book examines the significance of Adventist hermeneutics and the 1919 Bible Conference.

Delegates also found time to have fun. The diary of Clifton L. Taylor reveals that he went to downtown Washington, DC, on July 4 to celebrate American Independence Day. There, he "heard megaphone announcements of blow after blow as [Jack] Dempsey won the [heavy-weight boxing] World's Championship in three rounds." Little could the conference participants have realized how heated the theological discussions would become as they exchanged theological blows during the 1919 Bible Conference!

---

1. For a list, see Michael W. Campbell, "The 1919 Bible Conference and Its Significance for Seventh-day Adventist History and Theology" (PhD diss., Andrews University, 2008), 71n2.

2. Report of Bible Conference, July 1, 1919, 8.

3. M. C. Wilcox to A. G. Daniells, March 23, 1913, General Conference Archives.

4. General Conference Committee Minutes, April 15, 1918, 10, General Conference Archives.

5. Spring Council, General Conference Committee Minutes, April 29, 1919, 264; General Conference Committee Minutes, May 20, 1918, 36.

6. General Conference Committee Minutes, June 5, 1918, 46.

7. J. L. Shaw to W. A. Spicer, May 18, 1919, Secretariat General Files, Collection 21, Box 34 (#3316), folder "1919—Rice to 1919—Stahl," General Conference Archives.

8. General Conference Executive Committee Minutes, May 1, 1919, 273. See also Gilbert M. Valentine, "William Warren Prescott: Seventh-day Adventist Educator" (PhD diss., Andrews University, 1982), 507; Gilbert M. Valentine, *W. W. Prescott: Forgotten Giant of Adventism's Second Generation* (Hagerstown, MD: Review and Herald®, 2005), 276.

9. General Conference Committee Minutes, May 4, 1919, 283, 284.

10. General Conference Committee Minutes, May 5, 1919, 302, 303.

11. General Conference Committee Minutes, May 23, 1919, 325.

12. W. E. Howell to "Dear Brother," June 3, 1919, incoming correspondence, folder "Howell, W. E. 1918–1919," Ellen G. White Estate. It should be noted that M. L. Andreasen, for unknown reasons, did not attend the 1919 Bible Conference. It appears that F. M. Burg was not able to be present, and A. O. Tait was later asked to take over his presentations on the covenants.

13. Clifton L. Taylor diary, July 10, 1919 (a photocopy of the diary has been provided to the author). Taylor lists the record temperatures with numerous references to the "sizzling," "stifling," and "hot" temperatures.

14. For example, Daniells asked that part of a meeting not be transcribed into sixty typed pages. See Report of Bible Conference, July 16, 1919, 946. On another occasion, Daniells requested that a speech by Sorenson not be recorded, Report of Bible Conference, July 6, 1919, 246.

15. Report of Bible Conference, July 1, 1919, 9–16.

16. This is based upon the extant transcripts. See Campbell, "1919 Bible Conference," Appendix A.

CHAPTER 4

Adventist Hermeneutics

The crux of the 1919 Bible Conference would center on Adventist hermeneutics. The word *hermeneutics* comes from the Greek word *hermeneuo,* meaning "interpretation," or "how one interprets." This is the same Greek word translated as "explained" in Luke 24:27 (NIV), which was used when Jesus walked on the road to Emmaus with His disciples: "And beginning with Moses and all the Prophets, he *explained* to them what was said in all the Scriptures concerning himself" (emphasis added). Hermeneutics is the study of the principles involved in what Paul calls "rightly dividing the word of truth" (2 Timothy 2:15, KJV).

The 1919 Bible Conference was the first time in our Adventist past when "progressives" and "conservatives" were polarized against each other. While the roots behind this divide certainly go much deeper—in some ways back to such earlier conflicts, such as the 1888 General Conference Session or the controversy involving J. H. Kellogg and pantheism—the battle lines became much more clearly defined along hermeneutical fault lines. This chapter begins by discussing these hermeneutical battle lines.

Battle lines
The self-designated "progressives" were the dominant force at the 1919

Bible Conference. The General Conference president, A. G. Daniells, was an astute administrator who was careful not to let his own personal viewpoints dominate the discussions. Daniells had adopted the "new view" of the "daily" controversy (Daniel 8). Both Daniells and W. W. Prescott believed that truth is progressive, and therefore, the church should grow and deepen its understanding of that truth. At one point the progressive Prescott defended himself: "I would like to be understood as being a conservative. I thought I would have to proclaim it to you myself." He may have added that last sentence with a wry smile.[1] Yet at a later point, he felt he been attacked to the point that he refused to speak until a vote from the floor asked him to continue.[2] The "progressives" were joined by H. C. Lacey, a Bible teacher who would begin teaching at Washington Missionary College in the fall of 1919. At times, even the progressives could disagree quite strongly among themselves.[3]

A small, but assertive, group of traditionalists, or "conservatives," were concerned during the 1919 Bible Conference that their views were not being given adequate consideration. Some of the leading traditionalists included B. G. Wilkinson, E. R. Palmer, C. S. Longacre, and C. P. Bollman. Toward the end of the Bible conference, when Daniells remarked that he had not converted Bollman to his viewpoint, Bollman replied that neither had he been able to convert Daniells. This verbal repartee caused the audience to laugh.[4] Later, Palmer suggested that a committee of three (Sorenson, Longacre, and Wilkinson) present the "old view" about the "King of the North." Many of these same traditionalists were also concerned about some of the progressives who were advocating strong support for the doctrine of the Trinity (a topic that will be discussed in chapter 6).

A third group, although not necessarily present at the actual conference, included two vociferous critics, J. S. Washburn and Claude Holmes. They saw Daniells and Prescott as effectively leading the church in the wrong direction. Washburn and Holmes adhered to a rigid view of inspiration that emphasized the verbal inspiration not only of the Bible but also of Ellen G. White's prophetic writings. They advocated that both the Spirit of Prophecy and the Bible were free from all human error. As talks at the 1919 Bible Conference turned to issues related to revelation and inspiration (the subject of chapter 7), Washburn and Holmes became concerned that influential church leaders did not share their viewpoint. They published several angry pamphlets following the 1919 Bible Conference, describing it as a "diet of doubts." It does not appear that either individual was actually present during the 1919 Bible Conference, but it does seem that they were in the area at the time and sought information from other participants.[5]

Waging war

The 1919 Bible Conference covered a wide array of topics during the course of six weeks of presentations and discussions. The conference, therefore, provides a significant window into the development of Seventh-day Adventist theology. After all, Adventists, like other Christians, were confronted with a world that had changed rapidly and was continuing to do so. More specifically, as the broader American culture changed, many of these same movements were perceived by Adventists as signs of the end. Thus they were forced to reevaluate their role in this ever-shifting environment. The 1919 Bible Conference gives us insight into how Adventists were wrestling with these issues and with the new world in which they found themselves.

The 1910s were a tumultuous time for Seventh-day Adventist theology. How Adventists reacted to this time of change, particularly how they interpreted end-time events, gives rich insight into Adventist hermeneutics. Such issues were closely connected to Adventist identity. As the broader culture was perceived to be deteriorating, one way to respond was to become increasingly protective of traditional Adventist interpretations and traditions. As a consequence, discussions at the 1919 Bible Conference could become quite heated, with sharp words exchanged between participants. It was therefore imperative that they discuss their differences with the hope that this might help to bring mutual understanding.

The tension between tradition and openness, retreat and advance, is an important dynamic to understanding the overall 1919 Bible

Conference. The impulse toward openness allowed for discussions about differences and suggests that in some ways the church was maturing as different sides could present alternate ways of viewing an issue. On the other hand, some conferees felt threatened by new positions that might undermine more traditional viewpoints. This led to hesitancy and caution. Such dynamics were furthermore complicated by strong personalities, and, at times, feelings could get hurt. In order to avoid conflict, two procedures were put into place. First, an effort was made so that both sides could make presentations on a particular controversial topic. Second, issues that were especially divisive could not be discussed unless A. G. Daniells, the General Conference president, was present in the room.[6]

All of the issues discussed at the 1919 Bible Conference revolved in some way or another around the twin issues of how to interpret the Bible and Ellen White's writings. The conferees recognized that different approaches to inspired writings led to different outcomes. Thus, they acknowledged that principles of interpretation lay at the foundation of their differences.

The Bible and hermeneutics

The largest portion of the presentations and discussions at the 1919 Bible Conference centered upon the Bible and hermeneutics. In fact, the year 1919 marked seventy-five years since the Great Disappointment of 1844. A new generation of thinkers was at the helm of denominational leadership. Thus, traditional interpretative perspectives were being scrutinized.

Such scrutiny generally centered upon end-time events. As mentioned previously, World War I only heightened eschatological interest in the Second Coming. Adventists hoped, in a way similar to the Prophetic Conference Movement, that by drawing upon this anxiety, they would become better known to the general public. The geopolitical structure of Europe and Asia Minor forced Adventist exegetes to reexamine what they had taught prior to and during the war. While today many of these eschatological issues might seem to be somewhat obscure or dealing with peripheral matters, for those alive in 1919, they were serious hermeneutical matters over which a great deal of blood, sweat, and tears were shed.

The relationship between these eschatological issues and hermeneutics was crucial. Even C. M. Sorenson, who gave presentations on the ten kingdoms of Daniel 2 at the 1919 Bible Conference, observed how these issues might seem rather trivial: "Sometimes we may think these things do not matter much, that they are not essential to salvation. But they are vital. The interpretation of prophecy is essential to salvation in these last days. But there is a crusade of opposition against it, and an under-current among Seventh-day Adventists exists to put it away."[7]

Hermeneutical debates elevated the blood pressure of delegates. With so much at stake, C. P. Bollman pleaded with delegates to remember that some issues were not as important as some people might think they were. He called for tolerance:

> And here we might well dismiss the subject of the identity of the ten kingdoms, were it not for the reason that it affords such an excellent opportunity to make a plea for tolerance of opinion on this and other subjects not vital to our Adventist faith, nor necessarily destructive of good Christian experience. Why should one be considered a heretic, or be even suspected because he believes that the Alemani and not the Huns should be reckoned as one of the ten [kingdoms]? . . .
>
> Not one of these is fundamental, not one of them is one of the pillars of our faith.[8]

The issues connected to the 1919 Bible Conference were directly related to Adventist identity, even if not every issue warranted the same amount of attention. Once again, the two hermeneutical schools—progressives and conservatives—became evident as the conference progressed. In reality, they represented two different, polarized approaches to Scripture. The progressives focused on the context of each statement. They were open to making necessary revisions if they found something that was not necessarily correct, especially when it concerned historical details. The traditionalists emphasized a more literalistic way of interpreting inspired writings. They saw such changes as a threat, particularly since some of these conservatives embraced verbal inerrancy, according to which inspired writings do not have mistakes—even minor ones.

Principles of interpretation

The closest the Bible Conference came to discussing and defining hermeneutics was a presentation outlining principles of prophetic interpretation. This presentation was led by Milton C. Wilcox, who argued that if conferees understood the correct principles of prophetic interpretation, it would naturally lead to greater unity. Wilcox, sixty-six years old at the time, was one of the more mature conferees; he was also one of the more widely published authors and editors at this meeting.

In his presentation (and in subsequent discussions), Wilcox argued that the church must follow *principles* of interpretation for Bible prophecy. He argued: "Principles are greater than facts. They are to the student of the Holy Scriptures what the 'blue print' is to the builder." Such facts can't be interpreted by themselves in isolation. Instead, Wilcox argued: "Left to mere human conjecture, unguided by true principles of interpretation, men are liable to go astray in the placing of the fact."[9]

Wilcox provided a list of "great principles," but this list was not intended to be exhaustive, even if it was extensive. He listed twenty-one principles of interpretation: (1) unity of the Word; (2) one teaching; (3) law of first mention; (4) law of comparative mention; (5) law of full mention; (6) law of illustrative mention; (7) the Word paramount; (8) revealed, not reasoned out; (9) aid of the Spirit; (10) not of private interpretation; (11) conditional; (12) later lights; (13) nations and persons; (14) double prophecy; (15) great moral principles; (16) evidence is cumulative; (17) willingness to investigate; (18) reasons for prophetic delineation; (19) ending of great prophecies; (20) types and symbols; and (21) world dominion, not territory.[10] During later sessions, two more laws were added: L. L.

Caviness mentioned (22) the law of context, and H. C. Lacey added (23) the law of ancient Eastern usage.[11] The repeated appeal to "laws" suggests a Baconian mentality—an emphasis upon an orderly construction of reality—and the idea that if everyone agrees to the same principles, then all will naturally arrive at a consensus of truth.

During the discussions about "principles of interpretation," the "law of first mention" (principle 3) and the "law of context" (principle 22) drew the most attention among conferees. W. W. Prescott noted that "great care" was needed "when we take statements out of their setting that we give to them the meaning warranted by the setting."[12] L. L. Caviness noted that the "law of context" was the principle of interpretation most often violated. "I find myself that I have to fight against that. It is so easy to take something in the Bible or the Spirit of Prophecy and apply it as being a principle of truth for the present time, when maybe it has an application for the present time, but it had a stronger application at some other time."[13]

At the same time, there would be even stronger appeals to stand by traditional Adventist interpretations. In addition to these principles, M. C. Wilcox and L. L. Caviness expressed caution about the way in which a person interprets Scripture. An attempt should be made to first see what other Adventists "have taught or written, when we come to the study of the Scripture."[14] This appeal to tradition, by two leading traditionalists, expressed a desire to affirm the positions taken at the founding of the Adventist movement and to resist change, rather than embrace it.

While not necessarily a principle of interpretation, it should be noted that participants at the 1919 Bible Conference utilized a variety of different Bible translations available to them, and a number were conversant with biblical languages and were therefore comfortable sharing insights from Greek and Hebrew. H. C. Lacey, for example, noted that no translation of the Bible is able to perfectly convey the original meaning of the text. During the Bible conference, comparisons between the Authorized and Revised versions were common, for example.[15]

The group generally acted as though no Bible translation was infallible. They appeared to understand that language is inflected and that translations cannot perfectly convey the original emphasis. At another point during the meeting, H. A. Washburn (no relationship to J. S. Washburn) cautioned against reading the original text unless one was "very sure" that he understood the original language.[16] Thus the use of various Bible translations and biblical languages required care so as to not misuse valuable hermeneutical tools.

The topic of Bible translations also came up within the context of how to interpret the writings of Ellen G. White (the subject of chapter 7). During discussions on July 30 about the Spirit of Prophecy, William G. Wirth, a Bible teacher from Loma Linda, asked A. G. Daniells whether a conflict between different Bible translations could perhaps be solved by using Ellen White's prophetic writings. "I do not think Sister White meant at all to establish the certainty of a translation," observed Daniells. "I do not think she had that in mind, or had anything to do with putting her seal of approval on the authorized version or on the revised version when she quoted that. She uses whichever version helps to bring out the thought she has most clearly."[17]

Delegates agreed that the study of minute details of Scripture, including biblical languages, was not a replacement for a personal relationship with God. Those who knew biblical languages had a responsibility not to flaunt their knowledge or to give the impression that they were somehow superior to those who did not. Ultimately, it was the study of Scripture that was to be the supreme authority for settling doctrinal conflict, even if access to biblical languages and other tools for interpreting the Bible were important avenues for better understanding the original text. Those who learned these biblical languages were urged to utilize them, and those who did not know them were cautioned to take into account the various Bible translations available to them.

The "King James only" controversy did not arise during the 1919 Bible Conference. It would not be until 1930 that arch-conservative B. G. Wilkinson would publish *Our Authorized Bible Vindicated*, suggesting that many of the new, modern translations were based upon unreliable manuscripts because they were perceived as being tainted by modernism. Although Wilkinson was present at the 1919 Bible Conference, it was this concept of the inerrancy of Scripture, coupled with his perspective that contemporary scholarship was tainted by modernism, that laid the foundation for his later work.

Discussions about principles of interpretation, including the importance of context for hermeneutics and the different interpretations of words and phrases in their original languages, allowed participants at the 1919 Bible Conference to go into much greater depth than ever before about issues facing the church. Even though they embraced these principles, simply agreeing about them did not lead to the unity that they desired.

---

1. Report of Bible Conference, July 3, 1919, 192.
2. Report of Bible Conference, July 14, 1919, 758–762. F. M. Wilcox made the motion.
3. For example, Daniells told Prescott during the meeting: "No, I beg [your] pardon, but I will finish my statement and then I won't have to repeat it." Report of Bible Conference, July 6, 1919, 229.
4. Report of Bible Conference, July 17, 1919, 999.
5. Claude E. Holmes, *Beware of the Leaven (Doctrines) of the Pharisees and Sadducees*; Claude E. Holmes, *Have We an Infallible "Spirit of Prophecy"?* (n.p., 1921); J. S. Washburn, *An Open Letter to the General Conference*; J. S. Washburn, *The Startling Omega and Its True Genealogy*.
6. Report of Bible Conference, July 16, 1919, 904.
7. Report of Bible Conference, July 2, 1919, 101.
8. Report of Bible Conference, July 2, 1919, 74, 75.
9. Report of Bible Conference, July 2, 1919, 45.
10. Report of Bible Conference, July 2, 1919, 45–57.
11. Report of Bible Conference, July 2, 1919, 90.
12. Report of Bible Conference, July 3, 1919, 161.
13. Report of Bible Conference, July 2, 1919, 90.
14. Report of Bible Conference, July 2, 1919, 87, 88.
15. Cf. Report of Bible Conference, July 3, 1919, 160, 161; July 9, 1919, 470; July 13, 1919, 680.
16. Report of Bible Conference, July 3, 1919, 177; Report of Bible Conference, July 13, 1919, 628, 629, 666.
17. Report of Bible Conference, July 30, 1919, 1205.

Part 2

Major Issues

CHAPTER 5

Prophetic Interpretation

A variety of issues related to prophetic interpretation dominated the 1919 Bible Conference. Some of these issues, such as the identity of the ten kingdoms, the beginning and termination of the 1,260 day/year prophecy, and the identity of some of the seven trumpets resulted in a degree of consensus. Other issues, such as the "daily" and the identities of the king of the north versus the king of the south, resulted in heightened tensions. This chapter reviews these eschatological interpretative issues.

The ten kingdoms
A topic of extended discussion at the 1919 Bible Conference was the identity of the ten kingdoms mentioned in Daniel chapters 2 and 7. On the first full day of the Bible conference (July 2), Calvin P. Bollman gave a major presentation about the ten kingdoms that set the stage for subsequent discussions on the topic. The main contention centered on the identity of one of the ten kingdoms and the date for the rise of the papal horn.

Adventists have traditionally identified the successive metals of the image of Daniel 2 as signifying successive world monarchies: gold (Babylon), silver (Media-Persia), brass (Greece), and iron (Rome). The feet of the image are composed of iron and clay, and the toes are kingdoms that will never again be reunited. In Daniel 7, there is a beast with ten horns. Adventists believe that the toes of Daniel 2 and the horns of Daniel 7 are parallel symbols of the same thing. It was the identity of these "ten" toes and horns that was at stake for Adventist prophetic exegetes at the Conference in 1919.

Bollman was reluctant to give this talk because there were others present, he said, who were "just as familiar with the subject as I am." He added that although Daniel 2 was the natural starting point for examining this topic, the text did not explicitly refer to the "ten" toes as "kingdoms." "To me," he added, "it has for many years seemed unwise to say that in this prophecy the ten toes represent the ten kingdoms, for it is nowhere so stated in the Scriptures." The text did, however, state that the toes of the image would be divided and never again reunited. Bollman affirmed that Daniel 7 mentions " 'ten horns out of this kingdom [which] are ten kingdoms that shall arise.' Here we are on solid ground as far as the number ten is concerned."[1]

Bollman brought five lists of the ten kingdoms from four key sources. The first list came from Uriah Smith in his landmark work, *Daniel and The Revelation*. The second list came from *Notes on the Book of Daniel* by the Presbyterian amillennialist Dr. Albert Barnes (1798–1870). The third list came from an unnamed Roman Catholic source. The last two lists came from E. B. Elliott (1793–1875), whose *Horae Apocalypticae* was referred to more than any other non-Adventist book at the 1919 Bible Conference. Elliott's first list was for the fifty-seven years before A.D. 533, and the second was a list for the kingdoms after A.D. 533. The only difference between these two lists was that the Heruli replaced the Lombards after A.D. 533.[2]

For Bollman, the core question was determining the time when the "little horn" arose. According to him, the fulfillment of this prophecy validated Adventism's historicist approach to Bible prophecy. He added that some interpreters pointed to Paul's day as the beginning of the Roman papacy. Such persons traced its earliest origins to the "evil principle of self-exhaltation [sic] to which he [Paul] referred in" 2 Thessalonians 2:3–8. However, according to the prophecy, the ten kingdoms would be in existence by the time the little horn (the papal power) arose, and this "could not have been earlier than the first letter or decree of Justinian upon this subject, March 25, 533." This last, or eleventh, horn (the little horn) had to "be a real, tangible, organic entity, not merely a principle." It had to be more than an abstraction. The correct timing for this prophecy was crucial for establishing the rise of the papacy.[3]

The "little horn" would "exercise real power." Bollman argued that there had to be a historical fulfillment because the papacy did not die. "The Papacy can not [sic] be assigned to an earlier date than 533," he stated, "and indeed we have until recently assigned it a date five years later, namely 538." Bollman suggested that the papacy had nothing to do with the overthrow of the Heruli. It had previously been inferred that the Heruli had been overcome because they were Arians, but instead, historical evidence showed that they remained heathen until after the overthrow of their kingdom. "In fact the more this matter is examined in the light of modern research, the more evident it becomes that the Heruli never had any standing in Italy in any other capacity than that of barbarian warriors acknowledging no allegiance to any local leader except as he might either give or promise rewards in the shape of lands, lute [sic, loot], and license."[4]

Prenier, a teacher at South Lancaster Academy, found the name "Heruli" problematic because this same word had been used to designate four different tribes.[5] A more accurate identification, according to Bollman, was to include the Lombards as the tenth kingdom instead of the Heruli. He also suggested, as an alternative interpretation, that the Heruli may have been replaced by the Bavarian kingdom.[6]

L. L. Caviness led the response to Bollman by noting that if the Heruli were replaced by the Lombards in the list of the ten kingdoms, it would not only be a change from the traditional Adventist identification of the ten kingdoms but also replace the traditional date of A.D. 538 for the rise of the little horn with a new date—A.D. 533.

With that, the debate shifted from one that centered on historical accuracy to one focused, instead, upon Adventist tradition and authority. Caviness appealed to the writings of Ellen G. White by noting that the pope changed the Sabbath. E. R. Palmer expressed similar concerns. "It seems to me that to bring that [date, 533,] too definitely within the 1260 year period, it involves us in serious difficulty at both ends [both A.D. 538 and A.D. 1798], and I think we [would] have a good deal of phrase adjusting and word adjusting in our literature relative to the Sabbath and the papacy to make the thing consistent with what actually took place before the 1260 years and afterwards."[7]

Even the more progressive H. C. Lacey appealed to tradition, stating that he tried "to adhere to our traditional view [A.D. 538]."[8] H. A. Washburn averred, "I do not feel free to abandon the dates 538 and 1798. . . . That is the only thing that gives me anything to begin with."[9] Others, including G. B. Thompson, W. W. Prescott, and W. T. Knox, reflected on the fact that the early Adventist pioneers were not infallible. The church must press on to "advance in the light." Tradition was not good enough for those who leaned toward the progressive camp.

This issue of timing led to a broader interpretive discussion about the use of the term *supremacy* of the Roman Catholic papacy. C. M. Sorenson found the term *supremacy* to be problematic because the papal ascendency was gradual and really did not reach its oppressive zenith of domination until A.D. 1100 to 1300, after which it then began to fade. "And yet you read in our books and hear in our sermons that in 538 the pope became supreme." An interpretative view like this one needed to be true to actual history.[10]

A related area of discussion centered on if and how the papacy had changed the Sabbath before A.D. 533. If the papacy changed the Sabbath before it was supposed to have risen (regardless of whether the date was 533 or 538), then this negated the entire prophecy. H. A. Washburn responded by arguing that the bishop of Rome was indeed a monarchical power by this earlier (533/538) date.[11]

Attempts to identify the Heruli mystery spanned a variety of methods. Bollman again affirmed, as he had at the beginning of the discussion, that the ten toes (and thereby kingdoms) were not identified in the Bible. The key, for Bollman, centered upon geography, but these discussions precipitated another serious discussion about what actually occurred during this time period.

The 1,260 day/year prophecy

The discussions about the ten kingdoms led naturally to a discussion about a closely related topic—the dates for the beginning and ending of the 1,260 days/years of papal supremacy. These dates may seem to be of minor importance to the twenty-first century reader, but the conferees in 1919 considered this issue important enough to fight over because their whole Adventist identity was linked to a historicist interpretation of Bible prophecy. Adventists have always affirmed the historicist approach to Bible prophecy, which meant that identifying problems regarding the accuracy of this prophecy potentially threatened traditional Adventist interpretative positions.

H. S. Prenier made an attempt to present his views on Friday, July 11, 1919. While it appears that he read from his notes, only the first few remarks of the introduction and the conclusion of his talk are extant in the Bible conference transcripts. Prenier apparently argued that A.D. 533 was the "*primary date* for the *commencement* of the twelve hundred sixty years of papal supremacy." The "five-year period" from 533 to 538 was a transition time, and therefore Adventists could safely hold on to the 538 date as reliable.[12]

Prescott responded that "great care" should be taken over the matter about this date. He was chagrined that Prenier in his presentation had used some of Prescott's own earlier material to contradict him. He counseled that they should review only the "facts" about what "actually happened" on those dates. Prescott pressed for firm historical evidence instead of assertions. Thus he felt that 533 and 1793 would be much more accurate dates for this prophecy.[13] He was careful to also affirm that he believed in the 1798 date, when the papacy was humiliated, as the ultimate conclusion of this prophecy.

History teacher H. A. Washburn dominated the last part of the discussion on this issue. Ultimately, it was a matter of timing, and Washburn stated that perhaps two interpretations were possible. The overthrow of the three kingdoms (the Heruli, Lombards, and

Ostrogoths) occurred either *before* or *after* the papacy was established. He believed it was impossible to prove when the Ostrogoths were overthrown, but the bottom line was that by 538 they were gone.[14] Therefore, based on his own historical research, he was most comfortable with the latter date of 538.

The seven trumpets

One of the last eschatological issues discussed at the 1919 Bible Conference concerned how to interpret the fifth and sixth trumpets of Revelation 9. Early Adventists expositors believed the fifth trumpet was fulfilled by the invasion of the Eastern Roman Empire by the Saracens, and that the sixth trumpet referred to the invasion of the Ottoman Turks.[15]

J. N. Anderson led the debate by arguing that 1299 was the ending point of the fifth trumpet and the beginning of the sixth trumpet. He built his view on Uriah Smith's interpretation of Revelation. Smith had argued that the Saracens—a nomadic, Arabian tribe living on the Sinai Peninsula, that did not have a centralized king until 1299—were the fulfillment of the fifth trumpet. Anderson's presentation resonated with other traditionalists at the 1919 Bible Conference. Prescott, however, was uncomfortable with Anderson's position. Wakeham questioned whether it might instead be "false exegesis," because of unreliable research that misapplied the actions of the Ottomans to the Saracens. In fact, Prescott rightly noted, this position came from William Miller and his contemporaries. For him, this was Adventist exegesis gone wrong by asserting tradition above solid historical research. He argued that the 1299 date was "discredited" and tried to downplay this fact by arguing that a specific date was unnecessary.[16] He did not feel that he could present his own research on the topic since he had not come to the Bible Conference prepared to discuss this issue.

While the date 1299 was not central to Adventist eschatology, the fact that Prescott was willing to ignore it does reveal something about his underlying hermeneutical approach. Prescott was more concerned about the interpretation of what had actually occurred than he was about finding a historical event to validate a previously held position. Prescott's hermeneutic was historical accuracy. In this way, the battle lines were drawn between the progressives and the traditionalists. B. G. Wilkinson, one of the leading traditionalists, asked for the conference to withdraw a vote of support for Prescott so that he (Wilkinson) could defend the 1299 date. Neither the vote, nor the discussion surrounding it, are extant in the Bible conference transcripts, and neither is Wilkinson's later presentation. Later on, there were brief discussions on this controversial topic, but no consensus appears to have been reached.

What is clear is that the debate focused more on the methodology of how Adventists derived their understanding of the date, which the conferees considered as more important than the actual date itself. It appears that Wilkinson felt threatened by the questioning of what he considered to be a vital point. This added one more strand of color to the unfolding drama of the 1919 Bible Conference. These dates were important, because they linked history to Bible prophecy, thereby confirming the accuracy of Bible prophecy and validating Adventist theology. Yet there remained still more controversial issues related to prophetic interpretation that would dominate the Bible conference.

The "daily"

One of these controversial issues related to prophetic interpretation concerned the "daily," or "continual," sacrifice (Daniel 8, 11, and 12). Although the issue of the "daily" was not formally addressed by a paper, the debate over its interpretation appears to have colored discussions at the 1919 Bible Conference. The topic of the "daily" arose as a serious issue between 1897 and 1910 because it had implications regarding how one should interpret the following statement made by Ellen White: "The Lord gave the correct view of [the "daily"] to those who gave the judgment hour cry."[17]

The topic was especially important for three persons, A. G. Daniells, W. W. Prescott, and H. C. Lacey, who were proponents of what came to be known as the "new view." It appears that Ellen White's counsel at the 1909 General Conference Session to stop arguing about the subject had, until 1919, curbed the debate somewhat. But it was still a sensitive enough issue at the time of the Bible conference that Daniells instructed that it not be discussed unless he was present.[18]

One delegate, H. C. Lacey, connected the importance of the "daily" to the doctrine of the sanctuary. He understood the ultimate destruction resulting from the taking away of the "daily" as an attempt to destroy the heavenly sanctuary.[19] Unfortunately, the rest of his presentation is missing from the record. W. W. Prescott brought up the topic during his devotionals. He highlighted Christ's reference in Matthew 24:15 to the "abomination of desolation" mentioned by Daniel. Prescott suggested that this "abomination" destroyed the "daily" or "continual" sacrifice when Jerusalem was destroyed. The Bible, not tradition, should carry the weight of interpretative authority, argued Prescott. Furthermore, he declared that the "daily" had a "double application" that applied to those living just before the second advent of Christ. This emphasis on the "daily" sanctuary ministry of Christ reinforced the Adventist understanding of the cleansing of the sanctuary. Thus, Prescott proposed, this "new" view of the "daily" actually strengthened traditional Adventist theology rather than threatening it.[20]

Prescott and Daniells shared with the delegates how they had arrived at their understanding of the "daily." It came as the result of careful study. Daniells credited Prescott with sharing the "new view" with him during the late 1890s. In fact, he prefaced his remarks by noting that God would overlook Uriah Smith's interpretative mistakes in the same way that He would for William Miller. The overall context of Daniel 8 compelled Daniells to acknowledge that the "new" view was correct.[21] He saw Ellen White's statement as an affirmation of the fulfillment of the 2300 day/year prophecy in 1844, not as the final word about how to interpret every detail of this passage. Even though Ellen White had counseled to cease hostilities about the subject, this did not mean that individuals should relinquish their positions. Such tactics showcase that both sides within Adventism, including "progressives" like Daniells, were actually quite conservative in their attempts to strive for orthodoxy. As charged as the topic of the "daily" might be, yet the most controversial eschatological topic to be discussed at the conference would be the "king of the north."

The king of the north

Identifying the "king of the north" versus the "king of the south" (Daniel 11) certainly captivated the attention of the delegates. Once again, as he had with the "daily," the General Conference president, Daniells, decreed that the "king of the north" versus the "king of the south" was not to be discussed unless he was present.[22] And when the issue did arise later, Daniells stopped transcription. Like the "daily," this issue was crucial mostly for its implications regarding the underlying hermeneutical issues dividing the delegates. The progressives affirmed that it was more important to understand the meaning of an event rather than the actual date, that Adventists should use the latest historical research, and that proof-texting should give way to a hermeneutical approach that allowed Scripture to interpret itself (or in the case of Ellen White, to let her own writings interpret her statements).

Belief in Christ's soon return, along with confidence in how Adventists interpreted other prophetic passages in Daniel and Revelation, created room for Adventist interpreters to come up with varying interpretations of Daniel 11. In the 1840s, William Miller had interpreted the "king of the north" as Rome.[23] Uriah Smith modified this view when he wrote *Thoughts on Daniel and The Revelation*, adding that the battle between the king of the north and the king of the south would become a "triangular war" with France.[24] By 1900 there was growing dissatisfaction with Smith's interpretation.

By the time of the 1919 Bible Conference, the topic was addressed in two presentations given by C. M. Sorenson, chair of the religion department at Washington Missionary College, and H. C. Lacey, who would start teaching there that fall. Sorenson believed that Turkey should be identified as the "king of the north." Lacey, by contrast, argued the "new view" that the papacy fit the description much better.[25] Unfortunately, these talks appear to have only fanned the flames of theological debate, and no real consensus was reached among the delegates.

At the conclusion of these two talks, Daniells pointed out that what was clear in Adventist eschatology were the prophecies of Daniel 2 and 7. These debates over how to interpret these prophecies opened the door for additional discussions about the Trinity and, especially, the prophetic writings of Ellen G. White.

---

1. Report of Bible Conference, July 2, 1919, 60, 61.
2. Report of Bible Conference, July 2, 1919, 65, 66.
3. Report of Bible Conference, July 2, 1919, 66, 67.
4. Report of Bible Conference, July 2, 1919, 68–70.
5. Report of Bible Conference, July 2, 1919, 107.
6. Report of Bible Conference, July 2, 1919, 73, 99, 100.
7. Report of Bible Conference, July 3, 1919, 150, 151.
8. Report of Bible Conference, July 3, 1919, 152.
9. Report of Bible Conference, July 3, 1919, 190.
10. Report of Bible Conference, July 3, 1919, 152–155.
11. Report of Bible Conference, July 2, 1919, 105.
12. Report of Bible Conference, July 11, 1919, 604, emphasis in original.
13. Report of Bible Conference, July 13, 1919, 661, 662.
14. Report of Bible Conference, July 13, 1919, 667.
15. Report of Bible Conference, July 17, 1919, 964–978.
16. Report of Bible Conference July 17, 1919, 988, 989.

17. Ellen G. White, *Early Writings* (Battle Creek, MI: Review and Herald®, 1882), 74, 75. For more background on this controversy, see Arthur L. White, *Ellen G. White: A Biography*, vol. 6 (Hagerstown, MD: Review and Herald®, 1986), 246–261; Jerry Moon, *W. C. White and Ellen G. White* (Berrien Springs, MI: Andrews University Press, 1993), 415–427.

18. Report of Bible Conference, July 16, 1919, 842, 904.
19. Report of Bible Conference, July 7, 1919, 279–281.
20. Report of Bible Conference, July 17, 1919, 952–963.
21. Report of Bible Conference, July 8, 1919, 412, 413.

22. For a discussion, see Michael W. Campbell, "The 1919 Bible Conference and Its Significance for Seventh-day Adventist History and Theology," (PhD diss., Andrews University, 2008), 142–144.

23. William Miller, *Evidence From Scripture and History of the Second Coming of Christ* (Troy, NY: E. Gates, 1838), 86; William Miller, *Miller's Works*, vol. 2 (Boston, MA: Joshua V. Himes, 1841), 87, 88.

24. Uriah Smith, *Daniel and The Revelation* (Washington, DC: Review and Herald®, 1944), 280, 281.

25. Report of Bible Conference, July 6, 1919, 208–228, 246–258.

Chapter 6

The Trinity

In addition to the wide range of eschatological issues raised during the 1919 Bible Conference, one controversial topic emerged right from the beginning of the meeting—the Trinity. This subject arose at two significant points during the 1919 Bible Conference.

The first was during W. W. Prescott's afternoon devotional on the "person of Christ." While his devotionals were intended to be Bible studies with a spiritual emphasis, Prescott was unable to resist broaching the controversial subject of the Trinity. In fact, he brought it up in his devotional talks the very first morning! He connected the eternity of the Son as one derived through His existence from the Father. He stated:

> There is a proper sense, as I view it, according to which the Son is subordinate to the Father, but that subordination is not in the question of attributes or of His existence. It is simply in the fact of the derived existence, as we read in John 5:26: "For as the Father hath life in himself, even so gave he to the Son also to have life in himself." Using terms as we use them, the Son is co-eternal with the Father. That does not prevent His being in the only-begotten Son of God.[1]

Prescott commented on Colossians 1:15–17 by observing that "we are 'in Him.' " He did not believe that this text proved that Christ was a created being.[2]

The discussion continued that afternoon when Adventist educator W. E. Howell asked Prescott to explain what he meant by the word *beginning*. In response, Prescott quoted John 1:3, observing "Not to teach that is Arianism." Those who listened readily perceived that Arianism was the teaching that Christ had been created by the Father at some point in the past. Prescott went on to explain that some influential church publications stated, "that the Son is not co-eternal . . . with the Father," and rhetorically asked: "Do we want to go on teaching that?"[3] If there was a response, it was not recorded in the conference minutes.

The second time the topic of the Trinity arose at the 1919 Bible Conference was four days later (July 6). When the issue resurfaced, the discussion was much more earnest. After morning presentations about the king of the north by C. M. Sorenson and H. C. Lacey (each presenting opposing viewpoints), the afternoon discussion was originally scheduled to focus on the identity of the ten kingdoms. Instead, it became a debate about the Trinity when M. C. Wilcox asked Prescott a question about the Trinity. Another delegate, T. E. Bowen, pressed the issue, asking Prescott whether or not Christ had a beginning. More specifically, Bowen expressed skepticism that it was even possible to comprehend such a beginning detached from the idea of "eternity."[4]

Responding to Bowen's question, Prescott asked him to explain "where in the Scriptures it is taught that Christ had a beginning"? Bowen replied that the Scriptures "speak of His being the only begotten son." Prescott stated that this did not necessarily "fix any beginning." At this point, Lacey came to Prescott's defense by arguing that there never was a time when Jesus did not exist. "His existence spans eternity," Lacey affirmed. Caviness then challenged both Prescott and Lacey by stating that he had difficulty accepting the idea of Trinitarianism. Instead, he suggested that a semi-Arian view of Christ's sonship—meaning that the Son originated from the

Father "somewhere away back in eternity"—was perhaps a better approach that would be faithful to Scripture.[5] At this point in the discussion, Daniells asked that his comments not be transcribed.

Up to this point, the conversation had centered upon the exegesis of the word *begotten*. The Bible conference consisted of at least two groups who differed on their approach to Adventist hermeneutics. One group, the self-styled "progressives," led by Lacey and Prescott, articulated a much more open approach to Adventist theology. By way of contrast, a second group included archconservatives such as Bowen and Caviness, who represented a much more traditionalist approach. At the same time, it is important to note that many within both camps were very impressionable to the rising Fundamentalist movement with its emphasis upon traditional church teachings such as the virgin birth of Christ and the atonement of Christ on the cross.

Although there was essential unity on many core issues of the faith, there were other issues where there was some variety—specifically, issues related to revelation and inspiration. Some of the more traditionalist conservatives at this meeting would push for an Adventist hermeneutic that embraced what effectively became known in Fundamentalist circles as "inerrancy." There was certainly some fluidity between these different hermeneutical camps, and they even agreed on many aspects of Adventist identity, yet these opposing, underlying hermeneutical approaches would continually surface during the Bible conference. Later, these issues would become especially noticeable as they related to other issues dealing with Adventist prophetic interpretation, most memorably, with regard to the authority and interpretation of Ellen G. White's writings.

What is significant is that progressives (such as Prescott and Lacey) defended their position of accepting the Trinity based upon the exegesis of Colossians 1:15–17 and John 1:3. Bowen, in contrast, defended a semi-Arian position, but the precise reasoning behind his stance (and that of anyone who might have agreed with him) is not clear, because the transcripts at this point in the discussions have not survived. What is clear is that the progressives were driving home their point by doing serious research about the meaning of the actual Greek words.

There does not appear to have been a clear consensus on the issue of the Trinity at the 1919 Bible Conference. The reason seems to be far less about the main points of Adventist belief but had more to do, rather, with the fact that there was a deep hermeneutical divide that became self-evident during this meeting. This tension became particularly apparent when John Isaac expressed the following:

> What are we Bible teachers going to do? We have heard ministers talk one way. Our students have had Bible teachers in one school spend days and days upon this question, then they come to another school, and the other teacher does not agree with that. We ought to have something definite so that we might give the answer. I think it can be done. We ought to have it clearly stated. Was Christ ever begotten, or not.[6]

Daniells stated that what changed his mind from a previous non-Trinitarian perspective was reading Ellen G. White's statements affirming the full divinity of Jesus Christ from all eternity, as found in her classic work *The Desire of Ages,* published in 1898. He reassured the delegates that the conference would not force a vote on this topic at this meeting. Instead, he encouraged them to "think" about it and to continue to "go on with the study."[7] It is not possible at this point to know if the topic came up again in hallway discussions or other portions of the conference that were not transcribed. But it appears that the topic was eclipsed by other more pressing interpretative issues.

Perspective
The 1919 Bible Conference certainly did not resolve the issue of the Trinity, but it did mark a significant point of transition between the much earlier semi-Arian position advocated by Adventist thought leaders such as Uriah Smith during the 1870s and 1880s. During the 1890s a shift began to take place, in part due to a new generation of

Adventist theologians such as H. Camden Lacey, who spent a significant amount of time with Ellen G. White in Australia. If there was any doubt that Adventism was moving away from Arian positions, Ellen G. White made her position crystal clear when she wrote *The Desire of Ages* (1898). What the 1919 Bible Conference shows is that such issues continued to be scrutinized and debated four years after Ellen G. White's death. Although she made her position known, a theological shift on this topic took a great deal of time and careful Bible study. The denomination would continue to struggle with this issue during the rest of the twentieth century, even as it began to insert more Trinitarian wording into its hymns and statement of beliefs.

The topic of the Trinity at the 1919 Bible Conference also illuminates the hermeneutical divide within Adventist theology. While there was a great deal of consensus among conferees about core aspects of Adventist theology, that did not mean there were no hermeneutical differences. In fact, there appears to have been a significant hermeneutical divide between some of the more progressive delegates and the traditionalists at this meeting. This divide can be seen in multiple issues, including the Trinity.

While space does not allow discussion of all the other issues at this same meeting (which I have discussed elsewhere), those delegates who were more open and progressive tended toward accepting the full deity of Christ from all eternity. The more traditional Adventist expositors, however, viewed acceptance of the full divinity of Christ from all eternity as a compromise. I should also note that both sides tended to avoid using the term *Trinity* due to its associations with Roman Catholicism.

What is clear is that there was a general pattern as delegates discussed a wide range of issues. Those who adhered to a more progressive hermeneutic were the same ones who supported the full divinity of Jesus Christ and paved the way for the full acceptance of the Trinity in Seventh-day Adventist theology. Adventist historians have tended to paint the aftermath of the 1919 Bible Conference as one in which Adventist theology drifted heavily into Fundamentalism—especially with the demise of A. G. Daniells as the General

Conference president in 1922. Yet perhaps on this one particular issue, at least, those who were more progressive (most notably Prescott and Lacey) would eventually achieve a significant theological victory as the church gradually moved in their direction and later accepted Trinitarian statements in its Statement of Fundamental Beliefs throughout the twentieth century.

If this is the case, then Adventist hermeneutics were far more nuanced than has sometimes been recognized, and at times sought more moderate ground even as individuals continued to push toward the extremes. In the end, Adventist theologians agreed on far more than they disagreed on, and Adventist hermeneutics would continue to dominate discussions of Adventist theology to the present day.

---

1. Report of Bible Conference, July 2, 1919, 78.
2. Report of Bible Conference, July 2, 1919, 34.
3. Report of Bible Conference, July 2, 1919, 76, 77.
4. Report of Bible Conference, July 6, 1919, 232.
5. Report of Bible Conference, July 6, 1919, 232–236.
6. Report of Bible Conference, July 6, 1919, 245.
7. Report of Bible Conference, July 6, 1919, 244.

CHAPTER 7

Interpreting Ellen White

As these debates on various aspects of eschatology, the Trinity, and other topics unfolded, the delegates consistently appealed to the authority of Ellen G. White's writings. Her life and ministry, which had closed only four years earlier, was invoked repeatedly during various debates on biblical interpretation. The authority of her writings, whether they should be revised, and the nature of their inspiration were all subjects of great importance. The Bible conference would be the first time the denomination would discuss the nature and authority of her writings after her death. In order to appreciate the significance of these debates, it is important to situate them in the context in which participants at the 1919 Bible Conference explored her prophetic legacy. The first two dialogues in this area occurred during the main portion of the Bible conference (July 10 and 16). The last two occurred afterward (July 30 and August 1), as the Bible and history teachers continued to meet.

The first dialogue
The question of revising Ellen White's writings arose on July 10, when W. W. Prescott noted certain problematic statements in *The Great Controversy*. He compared statements in the 1888 and 1911 editions. He observed corrections of facts made by the author thanks to the help of

literary assistants and consultants. He highlighted at least seven problematic statements that had been either revised or removed from the 1911 edition.[1] The important point, for Prescott, was that all of these statements had to be harmonized with facts. He noted that while Ellen White was alive, "the author and editors recognized the propriety of making changes necessary when newly discovered facts were brought forward." He rhetorically asked whether such historical discrepancies destroyed confidence in her divine inspiration. No one, at least based on the extant transcripts, ever answered his question.

The discussion focused on an original letter written by Ellen White to a Conference participant, F. M. Wilcox. The content of the letter concerned revisions in *The Great Controversy*. The letter stated:

> When I learned that "Great Controversy" must be reset, I determined that we would have everything closely examined, to see if the truths it contained were stated in the very best manner, to convince those not of our faith that the Lord had guided and sustained me in the writing of its pages.
>
> As a result of the thorough examination by our most experienced workers, some changing in the wording has been proposed. These changes I have carefully examined, and approved. I am thankful that my life has been spared, and that I have strength and clearness of mind for this and other literary work.[2]

Wilcox continued by noting that the clearest statement Ellen White had made about the nature of her inspiration appeared in *Spiritual Gifts*, volume 1 (1858)—the very earliest edition of what would later become *The Great Controversy*. Even volume 2 of *Spiritual Gifts*, a book that was largely autobiographical, contained a number of testimonials vouching for the accuracy of her story and her use of sources. Any human shortcomings, Wilcox argued, could not discredit her divine inspiration. Even at this early period she "used the same care and the same means in making her work regarding the historical data correct," which confirmed that she was "an honest woman."[3] Despite the fact that some things might be "perplexing" in her writings, "the general spirit attending her life is evidence of her divine call from God as the messenger of this denomination." The stenographer noted several "amens" to this comment.[4]

During this first discussion, the conferees were hesitant to make Ellen White's writings an authority for historical facts. G. B. Thompson read a statement from W. C. White describing the revision process for *The Great Controversy*. This process highlighted Ellen White's instruction about how to find the best historical sources, verify quotations, and when inaccuracies were found, to submit proposed changes to her for approval. When the source for a specific quotation could not be found, her assistants were instructed to find another source making the same point.[5]

Although W. C. White was not at the 1919 Bible Conference (he was attending the double wedding of his twin sons), his close friend and colleague, D. E. Robinson, who was also one of Ellen White's literary assistants, did participate in the subsequent discussion. He noted that his thirteen years of working for Ellen White made him familiar with how she revised her writings. He said that, for example, he and C. C. Crisler "spent nearly six months in the study of *Great Controversy*." They spent time doing research in the libraries at Stanford University and the University of California, Berkeley.

Other delegates were concerned about how the revision process could affect the accuracy of Ellen White's writings. A. O. Tait noted that some of the "younger men have taught" that Ellen White's writings were equal to those of the Bible writers. This was contrary to what he remembered being taught by the early Adventist pioneers, especially G. I. Butler:

> Elder [James] White himself never spoke of the infallibility of Sister White's writings. But I do believe they are inspired; and if you allow Sister White herself to carry things along, and not a few men with extreme and fanatical ideas, we won't get into any trouble. But I have observed that the men who carried these extreme views have many of them left the faith. Sister White's teaching is always directing us to the infallibility of the Bible,

and never to herself or her writings as a standard. She is so much different from these others who have come forward.[6]

Similarly, William G. Wirth affirmed that he supported the views expressed that afternoon but complained that he had gotten "into trouble" because he would not teach that Ellen White's views of history were absolutely authoritative. He felt this information being discussed needed to get out to the teachers. Howell, as the education leader for the church, noted that the teaching of history would be discussed later on (the subject for chapter 8).

The real issue, according to veteran minister and administrator R. A. Underwood, went beyond the revision process or the accuracy of Ellen White's writings to the actual relationship of her writings and the authority of the Bible. Underwood argued that there were two similar and reinforcing extremes within the Seventh-day Adventist Church. On the one hand, there were those who placed "the Testimonies [to be] just the same as the Bible." This was the position that S. M. I. Henry, the famous convert from the Women's Christian Temperance Union during the 1890s, struggled with. A second extreme view placed Ellen White's writings as "a great telescope" which "magnified the word of God." From Underwood's perspective, this was the same as exalting Ellen White's writings *above* the Bible.[7]

A foundational concept for Underwood was that truth is progressive. He referred to the story of how the church developed its system for collecting church funds. An earlier plan, known as "systematic benevolence," was used for a time. As G. I. Butler and J. H. Morrison, two early stalwart ministers, studied the matter, they became convinced that the practice of giving a tithe (10 percent) was more biblical. Initially, there were some who opposed this on the basis that Ellen White had earlier endorsed the previous "systematic benevolence" plan. Underwood remarked that in denouncing those who took this position based on her earlier words, Ellen White "used the strongest language" he had ever heard her use. This was a classic example of how the "spirit of prophecy" brought unity to the church through a deeper study of the Bible.[8]

This first discussion affirmed that Ellen White had tried to make her writings as accurate as possible. Over her lifetime she continually revised her writings. She did not consider herself to be a final authority on historical details but used history to shed light on the Bible. The greatest proof of her inspiration was the overall trajectory of her life and ministry, which brought about church unity even as the church grew and changed positions on some issues. Some delegates, like A. O. Tait, recognized that Ellen White's writings were not the same as those of the Bible. The matter of inerrancy would be brought up again in later discussions about her writings.

Presentation by Daniells

This first discussion was followed by a formal presentation by A. G. Daniells on July 16. Unfortunately, only the first part of his talk is extant in the 1919 Bible Conference transcripts (at Daniells's request). At the outset of the meeting, Daniells stated that he had intended to gather statements to use for his talk that evening, but he was unable to do so due to his conducting a funeral earlier that day. He also expressed concern that some (presumably Claude Holmes and J. S. Washburn) accused him of being "shaky" about his confidence in the writings of Ellen White.[9]

Daniells related to the delegates his personal experiences with Ellen White. He first met James and Ellen White while in Texas in 1879, and later came to know her much better while in Australia and New Zealand from 1892 to 1900 (James had died in 1881). Yet, Daniells said, it was his personal experience with Ellen White during the conflict with Dr. John Harvey Kellogg, which resulted in Kellogg's departure from the denomination in 1907, that "stood out above all the rest" and bound him in "everlasting loyalty to that gift that God placed in the church."[10]

It seems best to presume that the rest of the talk that evening, which Daniells asked not be transcribed, most likely centered upon other aspects of his personal experience with Ellen White as the basis for his own confidence in her prophetic ministry. Daniells was selected as the chairman of the Board of Trustees that managed the

Ellen G. White Estate, and toward the end of his life, wrote a book defending her prophetic life and ministry. Whatever Daniells spoke about at that untranscribed meeting, it certainly became a catalyst for a question-and-answer session, known as the "round-table talk," that he had two weeks later with the teachers on July 30 and August 1.

The "round-table talk"

The most extensive discussion about the use of Ellen White's writings took place at the end of the main Bible conference, with the Bible and history teachers who were continuing to meet for another three weeks. The discussion, taking place some two weeks after Daniells's earlier talk about Ellen White, included only eighteen individuals (in contrast to the total of sixty-five who were present for the main Bible conference). The meeting was chaired by W. E. Howell, who had invited A. G. Daniells to come back to speak to the teachers about the use of the Spirit of Prophecy in teaching of Bible and history. From the outset of this meeting, Daniells indicated he preferred a "round-table talk" format to accommodate dialogue.[11]

The dialogue began by Daniells commenting on two general aspects of Ellen White's inspiration. First, he did "not want to create doubts" in the minds of those present. He had personally received testimonies from Ellen White, and he had found some things hard to understand. At times, he even had difficulty accepting her admonitions. He appeared somewhat defensive about accusations, presumably from individuals such as Holmes and Washburn, that he was undermining Ellen White's writings.[12] Some of this difficulty he attributed to battle scars from earlier power struggles with A. T. Jones and Dr. J. H. Kellogg at the beginning of his presidency.

Jones and Kellogg had fought Daniells for control of the church in a power struggle that ultimately alienated them from the denomination. Daniells noted that during this struggle, "a man" (presumably A. T. Jones) on the nominating committee had wanted him [Daniells] kept out of the presidency because he "did not believe the Testimonies were verbally inspired."[13] Later on during his talk, Daniells returned to problematic aspects of A. T. Jones's view of inspiration and Ellen White's writings. Daniells believed that his disagreement with Jones about verbal inspiration was the primary reason behind Jones's criticism. Daniells observed that Jones held to a strict, literal reading of Ellen White and would "hang a man on a word" from her writings. He reflected:

> I have seen him take just a word in the Testimonies and hang to it, and that would settle everything,—just a word. I was with him when he made a discovery,—or, if he didn't make it, he appeared to make it,—and that was that there were words in the Testimonies and writings of Sister White that God did not order her to put in there, that there were words which she did not put in by divine inspiration, the Lord picking the words, but that somebody had helped to fix that up. And so he took two testimonies and compared them, and he got into trouble. He [then] went on with Dr. Kellogg, where he could just pick things to pieces.[14]

The second area of concern for Daniells centered upon the way the church had presented the gift of prophecy. He was especially concerned about an emphasis upon the "physical and outward demonstrations." The story of Ellen White holding a large, heavy Bible outstretched for a long period of time perturbed him. "I do not know whether that was ever done or not. I am not sure. I did not see it. . . . I do not count that sort of thing as a very great proof." He wondered sometimes how much of this story was genuine versus what had "crawled into the story."[15]

While Daniells believed that supernatural phenomena accompanied her visions, especially in the early days of the movement, he did not believe this was really the best proof of her genuine inspiration. Instead, the greatest proof of her genuine prophetic gift was her overall life and contributions to the church, which could be seen in such areas as world evangelism, education, medical missions, and her overall spirit of sacrificial service.[16]

The first group of questions by the teachers centered upon the exegetical use of Ellen White's writings. Clifton Taylor, a Canadian

Bible teacher, posed the first two questions. He wanted to know whether Ellen White's explanations of Scriptural passages were authoritative, and whether or not those who differed about how to interpret a biblical passage should bring Ellen White's writings into the matter. Daniells replied that he had used Ellen White's writings to elucidate Scripture. Then he reflected, in what appears to have been an afterthought, that the Bible explains itself and must be understood through itself without resorting to the Testimonies (Ellen White's writings) to prove it.

He was concerned about those who think that the "only way" they "could understand the Bible was through the writings of the spirit of prophecy." At this point, J. N. Anderson interjected: "He also said 'infallible interpreter.'" It appears that Anderson was referring here to A. T. Jones and the challenges now facing the denomination regarding the authority and inspiration of Ellen White's writings due to the positions Jones had taken. Both Sorenson and Daniells believed that the view that Ellen White's writings were inerrant was an erroneous position that the church must avoid.[17]

A closely related group of questions, similar to these, centered upon the relationship of Ellen White's writings to the Bible. The earliest pioneers of Adventism had claimed that Adventism's unique doctrinal beliefs did not come from Ellen White's writings but, instead, resulted from an intense study of the Bible. It was crucial, according to Daniells, that Adventists derive their beliefs from the Bible itself. Ellen White's writings were meant to "enlarge our view." He insisted that Adventists should avoid being lazy about studying Scripture. "The earnest study of the Bible is the security, the safety of a man."[18]

The third major area of questions centered upon whether Ellen White's writings should be used "to settle historical questions." Daniells responded that although Ellen White certainly weaved history into her writings, she "never claimed to be an authority on history" or "a dogmatic teacher on theology." "I have always understood," he said, "that, as far as she was concerned, she was ready to correct in revision such statements as she thought should be corrected." This discussion became diverted into two major areas: (1) difficulties related to publishing Ellen White's book *Sketches From the Life of Paul* (1883), and (2) the controversy over the "daily" in Daniel 8, although Ellen White had repeatedly asked that her writings not be used to settle this controversy.[19] Both experiences, Daniells believed, were instructive for properly understanding Ellen White's writings.

C. A. Shull pushed Daniells further about his view of Ellen White's use of history. He pressed him on two specific points. First, Shull noted that the account of the apostle John being thrown into a pot of boiling oil was based on a *tradition*. When a student had brought this up to him in class, Shull had tried to use Ellen White's writings to prove it was historical fact. Shull asked Daniells rhetorically: "Was she [Ellen White] given a divine revelation that John was thrown into a vat of boiling oil?" Second, the ancient city of Babylon was taken, according to Ellen White, by "the turning aside of waters." Shull noted that modern scholars did not see it that way. Other teachers, including F. H. Williams and E. F. Albertsworth, resonated with these points Shull brought up. Albertsworth, in particular, noted how problematic it was when students tried to use Ellen White quotes to settle a particular point, instead of doing their own research.

Daniells believed that his experience with the "daily" controversy shed light on how one should properly understand this process:

> With reference to the historical matter, I cannot say anything more than I have said, that I never have understood that Sister White undertook to settle historical questions. I visited her once over this matter of the "daily," and I took along with me that old chart [by S. N. Haskell]. . . . I . . . laid it on her lap, and I took "Early Writings" . . . , and then I told her of the controversy. I spent a long time with her. It was one of her days when she was feeling cheery and rested, and so I explained it to her quite fully. I said, "Now here you say that you were shown that the view of the 'daily' that the brethren held was correct. Now," I said, "there are two parts here in this 'daily' that you quote. One is this period of

time, the 2300 years, and the other is what the 'daily' itself was."

I went over that with her, and every time, as quick as I would come to that time, she would say, "Why, I *know* what was shown me, that this period of 2300 days was fixed, and that there would be no definite time after that. The brethren were right when they reached that 1844 date."

Then I would leave that, and I would go on about this "Daily." "Why," she said, "Brother Daniells, I do not know what that 'daily' is, whether it is paganism or Christ's ministry. That was not the thing that was shown me." And she would go into that twilight zone right away. Then when I would come back to the 2300 years, she would straighten right up and say, "That is the thing we never can move away from. I tell you, you never can move away from that 2300-year period. It was shown to me that that was fixed."

And I believe it was, brethren. You might just as well try to move me out of the world as to try to move me on that question,—not because she says it, but I believe it was clearly shown to her by the Lord. But on this other, when she says she was not shown what the "daily" was, I believe that, and I take "Early Writings" 100% on that question of the "daily," fixing that period. That is the thing she talks about, and I take the Bible with it, and I take the Bible as to what the "daily" itself is.[20]

Daniells furthermore acknowledged that historians contradict one another. The fact that a person finds a problematic statement in Ellen White's writings should not "lead us away from the spirit of prophecy." She simply never meant for her writings to be used in that way. He added:

I do not believe that if Sister White were here to speak to you today, she would authorize you to take a historical fact, supposed to be a fact, that she had incorporated in the book, and put it up against an actual thing in history. We talked with her about that when "Great Controversy" was being revised, and I have letters in my file in the vault there where we were warned against using Sister White as a historian. She never claimed to be that. We were warned against setting up statements found in her writings against the various history that there is on a fact. That is where I stand. I do not have to meet it with students, and I do not have to explain myself in a congregation. I suppose I have it easier than you teachers do.[21]

Thus, if two historians of equal value contradict one another, the proper thing to do is to "bring up the authority that is in harmony with what we have."[22] When recently discovered historical facts do arise, the thing that is important is that she never "put infallibility into the historical quotations."[23]

On Thursday, July 24, Lacey gave a presentation, "The Aim, Scope, and Content of Our College Bible Studies." In this presentation, he challenged college Bible teachers, specifically, to become much stronger intellectually. He recommended that they make sure to cover the "inspiration of the Bible" in their courses. Bible teachers also needed to explain to their students the relationship of Ellen White's writings to the Bible: "The word of God is different from anything else. It is different from the Testimonies. It is verbally inspired, and the Testimonies are not, and do not claim to be, but the Bible does."[24]

William G. Wirth agreed with Lacey that the problem was that there were some teachers who taught that Ellen White was infallible with regard to historical details. Although the "progressives" were united in their belief that Ellen White's writings were not inerrant, Lacey's position shows that there was still diversity among them about exactly how they viewed inspiration, especially in relationship to the Bible. His comment revealed the growing sympathy in Adventist ranks for the verbal inspiration promoted by the Fundamentalist movement.

These conversations made it apparent that it was important for teachers to communicate their understanding of inspiration in the classroom. Lacey affirmed Daniells's earlier comments that the "value" of Ellen White's writings was "more in the spiritual light it throws into our own hearts and lives than in the intellectual accuracy in historical and theological matters. . . . Isn't the final proof of the spirit of prophecy its spiritual value rather than its historical accuracy?" Daniells believed this to be true. Lacey suggested that one way to address the problem of educating church members about inspiration would be to publish a "simple" pamphlet in a "straightforward style."

Other participants disagreed because enemies "would publish it everywhere." Wirth proposed: "I wish you general men would get something for us, because we [the teachers] are the ones that suffer." Even later during these "round-table" discussions, requests were made for similar resources, but nothing appears to have come about as a result of these requests. Perhaps it was felt that a published statement would be too controversial.[25]

The last major area of discussion during the first of two days of "round-table" interaction related to questions about health reform. In the transcripts, Daniells appears to be much more comfortable discussing these issues than he was in exploring the inspiration of Ellen White's writings. In fact, he told a story of a Scandinavian colporteur who tried to make Ellen White's counsels on health into a "blanket regulation" for his lifestyle. He tried to maintain a vegetarian diet in a place where fresh fruits and vegetables were scarce, if available at all.

When Daniells met this colporteur at a workers meeting, he was white as a ghost. "I went at him with all the terror I could inspire for such foolishness," he remarked. "When I got back to this country [the United States] I talked with Sister White about it, and she said, 'Why don't the people use common sense?'" Daniells emphasized the vital importance of understanding the original context in which Ellen White wrote a "testimony" in order to be able to apply her teachings in a balanced manner. "Sister White was never a fanatic; she was never an extremist. She was a level-headed woman. She was well-balanced." Ellen White wrote counsels about health to individuals in a wide variety of situations and in various states of health. The problem was "extremists" who either distorted her meaning or did not recognize historical context.[26]

At the conclusion of this session, Howell reflected that they had spoken "very frankly" with the teachers about the use of Ellen White's writings. Time did not allow them to cover all the topics they wished to address. Once again, Howell urged the teachers to help in "setting people straight on these things."

Additional questions

The "round-table" discussions continued on Thursday, August, 1. Daniells created the same kind of "round-table" environment as the previous day so that the teachers would feel comfortable asking questions.

Daniells began his remarks by noting that there were two views in Christendom regarding the inspiration of the Bible. One view, according to him, held that the Bible writers were allowed to state the truth as best they could in their own words. The second view was a word-for-word inspiration (along the lines of inerrancy). Daniells observed that honest, sincere persons held both positions and even had their followers with them at that moment. Howell pressed Daniells to focus his remarks on Ellen White's writings and their relationship to the Bible.[27]

The central question of this discussion was posed by C. L. Benson, at that time assistant secretary (director) of the General Conference Education Department. He argued that if there were historical uncertainties with regard to traditional Adventist interpretations, the "testimonies" were not meant to be ironclad interpretations about history or theology that could never be changed. Participants pressed him about whether there were some positions that were settled. Those delegates present were not about to let him off the hook too easily. Benson responded, "I think we could argue about the inspiration of the Bible—I was going to say till doomsday—till the end, and not come to the same view, . . . and all get to the same place at last."

He brought the point home more specifically about Ellen White: "I think more mischief can be done with the Testimonies by claiming their verbal inspiration than can [be done] with the Bible."

Daniells was careful not to state that he believed in the verbal (inerrant) position of the Bible. "It is no kind of use for anybody to stand up and talk about the verbal inspiration of the Testimonies, because everybody who has ever seen the work done knows better, and we might as well dismiss it."[28]

The issue of inspiration just would not go away. M. E. Kern probed Daniells further. He was not so certain "that we are all agreed on this question." He asked Daniells to "get down to bedrock" on this issue. Thompson suggested that the reason this topic was controversial was "wrong education." "If we had always taught the truth on this question, we would not have any trouble or shock in the denomination now. But the shock is because we have not taught the truth, and have put the Testimonies on a plane where she says they do not stand. We have claimed more for them than she did."[29]

Thompson's brief comment would afterward become one of the most famous statements from the 1919 Bible Conference. Only the passing of time, particularly after the transcripts were rediscovered, would the lens of hindsight perceive the wisdom of this statement about the importance of educating church members to have a healthy, balanced understanding of inspiration.

During this discussion, the primary issue facing the church related to the infallibility or inerrancy of Ellen White's writings. Daniells observed that James White, who passed away in 1881, had anticipated this problem and had tried to correct misconceptions about inspiration. "If that explanation had been accepted and passed on down, we would have been free from a great many perplexities that we have now," Daniells stated. Yet the issue was more than just a correct understanding. It also involved seeking ways to communicate an accurate understanding of this process of inspiration to church members. There were some, both young and old, who believed Ellen White was "word-inspired" and therefore "infallible." Daniells commented: "I suppose some people would feel that if they did not believe in the verbal inspiration of the Bible, they could not have confidence in it. . . . I am sure there has been advocated an idea of infallibility in Sister White and verbal inspiration in the Testimonies that has led people to expect too much and to make too great claims, and so we have gotten into difficulty."[30]

Even the charge of plagiarism, surmised Daniells, could have been avoided if "we had understood this thing as it should have been." Many of the challenges the church faced were tied to a faulty view of inspiration. After all, Ellen White never claimed verbal inspiration. Daniells concluded firmly: "I will say no more along that line."[31]

If the consensus was that Ellen White's writings were not inerrant, the discussion next turned to the question of whether she was infallible. Daniells asked his listeners if there was not a chance for the manifestation of the human in one who was the messenger of the Lord (a euphemism for Ellen White). If so, "then aren't we prepared to see mistakes?" He continued by reflecting on Ellen White's book *Sketches From the Life of Paul* (1883). He noted the claims about plagiarism made against it. He shared how he had read the book with E. R. Palmer and then compared it with the similar work of Conybeare and Howson and with Wylie's *History of the Reformation*, two well-known reference works in Adventist circles because Ellen White recommended them during her lifetime.

Both volumes were in Ellen White's library and had been referenced many times in her writings. Daniells continued,

> The poor sister [White] said, "Why, I didn't know about quotations and credits. My secretary should have looked after that, and the publishing house should have looked after it."
>
> . . . There I saw the manifestation of the human in these writings.[32]

The "round-table" reflected on other examples of changes made in Ellen White's books. One of these was her reference to the ceremonial law, which had been removed from her newer work *The Acts of the Apostles* when it superseded *Sketches From the Life of Paul*.

C. M. Sorenson observed that it was Ellen White's philosophy of history, and not the details, that was important. Minor details and variations might come up, but it was ultimately her overall philosophy of history and how God's hand worked through human history, that was truly important. The danger was that some people might begin to try dividing between what was inspired versus other content that was not. This was the same problem Prescott had confronted with A. R. Henry, Review and Herald publishing house manager from 1886 to 1897. Henry had tried to determine what was "authoritative" in her writings versus what was not. To make such delineations was positively dangerous, according to Prescott. Either she was fully inspired or not. Furthermore, Prescott felt that great mistakes had been made for years in how Ellen White's writings were handled for commercial purposes. At times, this led to their hasty publication and increased the chances of mistakes in her books.

Daniells concluded the "round-table" discussions feeling optimistic, noting "we have made a wonderful change in nineteen years." He went on: "Fifteen years ago we could not have talked [about] what we are talking [about] here today. It would not have been safe."[33] Issues about inspiration and the authority of Ellen White's writings repeatedly came up in the church. This, Daniells believed, was evidence that church members valued her writings. He left the teachers by urging them to use care and common sense as they taught about these subjects in the classroom.

Hermeneutical perspective

The discussions about Ellen White and inspiration showcase the reality that there were two contrasting positions about Adventist hermeneutics during the Bible conference. The first position was that of the self-styled "progressives," who knew from personal experience that Ellen White's writings were not inerrant nor was she infallible. They did, however, exhibit some variation about what "verbal inspiration" meant with regard to the Bible as well as on the specific relationship between her writings and the Bible. Lacey, for example, seemed to differentiate somewhat between the inspiration of the Bible and that of Ellen White's writings.

The main difference between the "progressives" and the

"traditionalists" concerned the verbal inspiration of Ellen White's writings. The "traditionalists," who tended to be much younger and most of whom had not worked closely with Ellen White, believed that Ellen White's writings were verbally inspired and thus inerrant. This appears to have been the position of critics such as J. S. Washburn and Claude Holmes, who, although they were not present during the meetings, regarded the writings of Ellen White as both infallible and equal in inspiration to Scripture. The progressive Lacey, by way of contrast, argued that both Ellen White's writings and the Bible were verbally inspired, although they were not inerrant. Thus, two camps emerged, even if there were some variation and blending of views by some participants.

---

1. For a list of these statements, see Michael W. Campbell, "The 1919 Bible Conference and Its Significance for Seventh-day Adventist History and Theology" (PhD diss., Andrews University, 2008), 145.

2. Ellen G. White to F. M. Wilcox, Letter 56, 1911, Ellen G. White Estate. The letter is mentioned in Report of Bible Conference, July 10, 1919, 558.

3. Report of Bible Conference, July 10, 1919, 559.

4. Report of Bible Conference, July 10, 1919, 560.

5. Report of Bible Conference, July 10, 1919, 561 and onward.

6. Report of Bible Conference, July 10, 1919, 564.

7. Report of Bible Conference, July 10, 1919, 566. See also S. M. I. Henry, "My Telescope," *Gospel of Health*, Jan. 1898, 25–28. It is important to note that when Henry used this metaphor, she made the point that Ellen White's writings do not add anything to the Bible or change it, just as a telescope does not add to or change anything in the starry heavens. This only allows for objects to be seen more clearly. Underwood took the word *magnify* to mean that her writings were a lens through which to interpret the Bible, thus putting Ellen White's writings as the controlling norm over Scripture.

8. Report of Bible Conference, July 10, 1919, 566, 567.

9. Report of Bible Conference, July 16, 1919, 942, 943, 949.

10. Report of Bible Conference, July 16, 1919, 944.

11. Report of Bible Conference, July 30, 1919, 1187.

12. Report of Bible Conference, August 1, 1919, 1255.

13. Report of Bible Conference, July 30, 1919, 1188, 1189, 1223.

14. Report of Bible Conference, July 30, 1919, 1208, 1209.

15. Report of Bible Conference, July 30, 1919, 1190–1193.

16. Report of Bible Conference, July 30, 1919, 1190–1193.

17. Report of Bible Conference, July 30, 1919, 1194, 1195.

18. Report of Bible Conference, July 30, 1919, 1196, 1197. For an overview of the

development of Adventist beliefs and their relationship to the ministry of Ellen G. White, see Alberto R. Timm, "The Sanctuary and the Three Angels' Messages 1844–1863" (PhD diss., Andrews University, 1995).

19. Report of Bible Conference, July 30, 1919, 1202–1205.

20. Report of Bible Conference, July 30, 1919, 1206, 1207. Daniells's reference to the "twilight zone" was an obvious reference to Ellen White's advanced age and accompanying mental decline.

21. Report of Bible Conference, July 30, 1919, 1207.
22. Report of Bible Conference, July 30, 1919, 1208.
23. Report of Bible Conference, July 30, 1919, 1212.
24. Report of Bible Conference, July 24, 1919, 1175.
25. Report of Bible Conference, July 30, 1919, 1213, 1214.
26. Report of Bible Conference, July 30, 1919, 1216–1222.
27. Report of Bible Conference, August 1, 1919, 1227, 1228.
28. Report of Bible Conference, August 1, 1919, 1233, 1234.
29. Report of Bible Conference, August 1, 1919, 1238, 1239.
30. Report of Bible Conference, August 1, 1919, 1241.
31. Report of Bible Conference, August 1, 1919, 1242, 1243.
32. Report of Bible Conference, August 1, 1919, 1243, 1244.
33. Report of Bible Conference, August 1, 1919, 1243, 1256.

Chapter 8

Teaching History and Training Pastors

Another noteworthy aspect of the 1919 Bible Conference was the rise of professional historians. Prior to the 1919 Bible Conference, there were those who wrote theological or apologetic history. But now, for the first time, the denomination recognized a new cadre of professional historians, which in turn corresponded to the professionalization within academia in general. This forgotten generation of Adventist historians made their debut at the 1919 Bible Conference. Another significant aspect of the 1919 Bible Conference was General Conference president A. G. Daniells's clarion call for the professional training of Adventist ministers. He envisioned a time when better-trained pastors would give more credibility to the spread of the Adventist message. This clarion call would lead to the professionalization of Adventist historians and the rise of intentional theological education for Adventist ministers.

Teaching history
The 1919 Bible Conference provides an excellent window into the development of Adventist historical consciousness. After the death of Ellen G. White (discussed in chapter 2) and the other early Adventist

pioneers, Adventists sensed that the field of history was becoming more professionalized and that they needed to keep up with the times as part of a conscientious effort to remain historically accurate. This sense of historical consciousness has always been a hallmark of Adventist identity.[1] With a new generation of historians on the scene, how to describe the past became an important matter of discussion among the Bible and history teachers.

The first presentation about teaching history was given by W. W. Prescott on July 21, the last Monday before the conclusion of the formal Bible conference. Prescott used his devotional talk that day to discuss the relationship between teaching the Bible and teaching history. Both subjects, he believed, were part of one great whole. He clarified that "the Bible throws more light on history than history throws on the Bible." His point was that both the Bible and history reveal God's ultimate purpose for earth. Thus "The Bible and history will complement each other and make a complete whole."[2] History should reveal God's guiding hand.

The most important talks about history are undated, presumably from the time during the Bible and history teachers' meetings. The first presentation was given by E. F. Albertsworth, a history teacher at Washington Missionary College, and the second by C. L. Benson, assistant director of the General Conference Education Department. (Benson's talk references Albertsworth's, so it must have occurred at some point afterward.)

In these talks, both Albertsworth and Benson mention the training they each had received in the "historical method." Albertsworth had studied at George Washington University and, in addition, had taken a graduate seminar in the historical method at Johns Hopkins University. Both Albertsworth and Benson mention that a chief problem for teachers was their inability to find primary sources. Many teachers served at schools with inadequate libraries, and the lack of access to quality materials was the "greatest handicap" they faced.

Teachers should also learn languages, they declared. For example, some teachers should learn Latin in order to access primary sources of the early Christian church. Albertsworth envisioned a time when Adventist specialists could be sent to Europe to study in the "great archives" there. Some of those present remembered J. N. Andrews, who had learned different languages and conducted research and thereby was better equipped to explain and defend the Sabbath truth. "He set a worthy example to our history teachers," remarked W. E. Howell.[3]

In his presentation, Albertsworth concentrated on historiography—the study of history. He provided a broad overview, extending from the ancient Greek historians, such as Herodotus, Thucydides, Polybius, Xenophon, on to Eusebius, the Middle Ages, and up through the Renaissance. Albertsworth argued that historical consciousness developed over time. This historical consciousness allowed historians to critically evaluate historical sources.

History students must be taught how to evaluate the reliability of a document by asking questions: Does the document contradict itself? Did the author witness the event being described? How trustworthy is the writer? He suggested several tests for determining reliability. As an example, Albertsworth cited the writings of J. H. Merle d'Aubigné, who was not a professional historian even though he wrote extensively about the Protestant Reformation. "I do not suppose any writer was under a greater bias than d'Aubigné," he stated. "We do not see him quoted so much anymore." The implication was that Adventist scholars should use more reliable and less biased historical sources in their historical writing.[4]

Benson spoke about the application of the principles of historic method to our own teaching work. "I have thought for a long time" he stated, that historical research work is "the weakest place in our denomination." He feared that if challenged, Adventist historians would not be able to provide solid historical evidence for their positions. Adventist ministers especially needed to give credible sermon illustrations and avoid making a "hodgepodge of history."[5]

Benson urged teachers to take advantage of the opportunity to do research in various archives while they were in Washington, DC, attending these meetings. Furthermore, he urged that Adventists should form "some sort of society" of historians to help "stimulate" cooperative research. In this Benson was fifty years ahead of his time; it would not be until the 1970s, that the Association of Seventh-day Adventist Historians was formed.

Other concerns Benson had centered on the quality of sermons being preached from Adventist pulpits. Pastors needed to learn how to do thorough research when preparing their sermons so that they had credibility. Another area of concern was the rise of higher criticism. Such concerns within Adventism hearkened back to Dr. John Harvey Kellogg, whom Benson perceived as pushing higher criticism. He assured educators that they could embrace the historical method without losing their faith. Benson and Albertsworth cast a broad vision for historical scholarship in the Seventh-day Adventist Church—one that they believed would make Adventism more credible in the future.

Theological education
One lasting contribution of the 1919 Bible Conference was the broad vision for the training of Seventh-day Adventist ministers voiced by A. G. Daniells and W. W. Prescott, two of the most visible personalities at the conference. Once again, as a more professional clergy was being developed within America at large, Daniells sensed that Adventists needed professional ministers who were trained and who could keep up with the times. This vision would have a profound impact contributing to the rise of a professional pastorate within Adventism.

The first hint about the need for increased ministerial education was made by W. W. Prescott during his devotional talk on July 21. He referred to a suggestion circulating at that time that a pastor should have fourteen years of education (that is, two years of training beyond high school) as a requirement for ordination. Obviously, there was a clear sense that the church needed to raise the standard for Adventist clergy in a move that would parallel efforts being made by other conservative Christian denominations at that time.[6]

A. G. Daniells made the most direct statement about the need to raise the standards for Adventist ministerial education. He gave a clarion call for a higher standard of ministerial education on August 1—the same day that he met with Bible and history teachers to discuss the Inspiration of Ellen G. White's writings. In this presentation, he set forth clear goals for training pastors. After his intense dialogue as part of the roundtable discussion on that day, he shared his burden for ministerial education and what such ministerial training should look like.

Daniells's vision for ministerial education would eventually result in a broad increase in ministerial training. However, graduate training of pastors would not begin for another fifteen years (1934), when the Advanced Bible School (now the Seventh-day Adventist Theological Seminary) was formed. In 1919, Daniells sensed this need and set forth a vision with the goal of fulfilling it. He estimated that nearly half of those present at the 1919 Bible Conference were involved in pastoral education in some way. He believed that the teachers had a key role in the development of pastoral training.

"I think, brethren," urged Daniells to the Bible and history teachers, "that among all the vocations in the world, that of the minister is the highest and most sacred, and calls for the greatest care on the part of those who enter it."[7] As a church administrator, Daniells was perturbed by the low quality of graduates he observed starting out in ministry. Such individuals, despite having studied, appeared to him to be poorly prepared for the grueling task of pastoral ministry.

Teachers had a responsibility not only to provide theoretical training but to prepare pastors for the practical demands of ministry. In this way, future ministers would learn how to model ministry. Both inside and outside the classroom, teachers should model the life of a minister. Core values that Daniells felt ministerial students especially needed included honesty, sincerity, integrity, and good judgment. Training pastors was both a responsibility and an opportunity for the teacher to go beyond teaching mere theoretical knowledge.

Prospective ministers should be studious and learn to work hard. It went without saying that teachers should recommend good books. In order to balance the wide-ranging responsibilities of pastoral ministry, "regularity in their habits of study, working and living" (or as Daniells later put it, the "value of time") was essential. "A great deal of time is lost and effort wasted by [the] lack of [such] a program." The most important book for ministerial training, of course, was the Bible; it should be "supreme." Scripture "contains great power," and students should let its "regenerating influence" affect their minds and hearts.[8]

Another area for ministerial training included more instruction in how to preach. First of all, Adventist preaching needed to be more Christ-centered; this, alone, would transform the way the denomination's ministers preached. As an example of such preaching, A. G. Daniells recalled a sermon illustration by William B. Riley that Daniells had heard during a visit to Riley's church in Minnesota. In his sermon, Riley told the story of an unlearned preacher who spoke so clearly about the parallel between the *sun* and the *Son* of God. Daniels emphasized that this parallel was both effective and an easy way to share a basic truth from God's Word. Most important of all was that the preacher expound God's Word.[9] What was clearly needed, Daniells urged, were expository sermons in Adventist pulpits.

These goals signaled a new direction for Adventist ministerial education. While his goals were not immediately realized, Daniells devoted the rest of his career to helping achieve them. In 1922, when he stepped down as General Conference president, he began to shift his attention to ministerial education. Then, in 1926, he organized the General Conference Ministerial Department. The core purpose of this organization was to provide resources for Adventist pastors so that they could become more effective.

Perspective

A significant component of the 1919 Bible Conference was the professionalization of Adventist historians and ministers. This impact can be seen in three important ways. First, the Bible was emphasized as a central component of both a philosophy of history and of Adventist ministerial education. Historians served a useful purpose by bringing credibility to the promulgation of the Adventist message. Similarly, pastors needed to be rooted in a biblical, Christ-centered approach in their preaching and ministry.

Second, a new generation of professional historians showed the importance of using primary sources. This kind of research should also characterize Adventist preaching as ministers should use credible sources in their sermons. Finally, the professionalization of Adventist educators meant higher standards for Adventist ministerial education.

While it would take some time before these dreams would be realized, the seeds for such plans were clearly articulated during these pivotal discussions held in conjunction with the 1919 Bible Conference. All of these areas, and more, showcase how church leaders recognized during these meetings the long-term strategic value that educators played in the church.

---

1. For a recent treatment of Adventist historical consciousness, see Gabriel Masfa, "A Study of the Development of Seventh-day Adventist Historiography" (PhD diss., Adventist International Institute of Advanced Studies, 2018).

2. Report of Bible Conference, July 21, 1919, 1117–1132.

3. Report of Bible Conference, August, 1, 1919, 1302.

4. E. F. Albertsworth, "Historical Method," n.d., 17, 18, in Report of Bible Conference, August 1, 1919, 1297, 1298.

5. C. L. Benson, "The Application of the Principles of Historic Method to Our Own Teaching Work," n.d., 1, 2, in Report of Bible Conference, August 1, 1919, 1274, 1275.

6. Report of Bible Conference, July 21, 1919, 1132.

7. Report of Bible Conference, August 1, 1919, 1261.

8. Report of Bible Conference, August 1, 1919, 1259, 1260.

9. Report of Bible Conference, July 3, 1919, 130, 131.

Part 3

Postlude

CHAPTER 9

Aftermath

Assessments of the 1919 Bible Conference during the twentieth century have varied considerably. Some of the earliest reactions were quite varied. Some called the meeting a "diet of doubts," although official published reports were extremely positive. After a time, the 1919 Bible Conference was all but forgotten, becoming just one of many conferences held by the denomination that year. Yet during the 1920s, a denomination that was, at first, flirting with Fundamentalism would shift toward a one-sided love affair. An older generation of church leaders, many of whom had a much more moderate view of Inspiration that avoided inerrancy and who had worked closely with Ellen G. White, passed from the scene of action. At times, some of these more moderate thought leaders were ignored or ostracized. What is clear is that the 1919 Bible Conference marked a key moment during this pivotal period.

The significance of the 1919 Bible Conference would not be realized until the transcripts were rediscovered five decades later. By that time, new struggles about the Inspiration of Ellen G. White meant that when these candid 1919 discussions surfaced, particularly the ones dealing with Ellen G. White's writings described in chapter 7, it was nothing short of explosive. A new generation of progressive Adventists recognized that soon after Ellen G. White's death, church thought leaders had been asking those who adhered to the errancy of her writings probing questions about how to interpret her writings, the nature of their authority, and other problematic aspects of the errancy position.

This chapter reviews some of the immediate reactions to the conference, followed by a brief synopsis about how the transcripts were rediscovered.

Immediate reactions

Although some of the discussions during the 1919 Bible Conference apparently could get quite heated at times, by the time the main Bible Conference concluded with a special "devotional service" on Sabbath, July 19, twenty-five of the sixty-five delegates who testified publicly expressed deep appreciation for the fact that the denomination had called for such a Bible conference. These testimonies came from both progressives and traditionalists who expressed satisfaction at what they had learned while they were together.

Some, such as W. W. Prescott, described the conference as a "turning point" in the denomination. Several persons stated that the Bible conference changed their life—challenging them to become more Christ-centered in their teaching and preaching. Daniel Kress, an Adventist physician, recalled his initial hesitation at having a meeting where different viewpoints were presented, but now that the main part of the Bible Conference was over, he believed that it had been a great blessing. Similarly, W. E. Howell, one of the original organizers of the Conference, stated that the Bible Conference exceeded his expectations.[1]

Another common characteristic of the testimonials was expressions of increased confidence and appreciation for the prophetic writings of Ellen White. John Isaac, a Bible teacher at Clinton Theological Seminary, mentioned that his confidence in the writings of Ellen G. White had increased during the Bible conference. O. M. John, associate secretary of the General Conference Education Department, commented that the things he learned had already helped him counsel a young person experiencing "doubts" about "the Inspiration of

Aftermath

the Bible and Testimonies [Ellen G. White's writings]."[2] Such candid conversations resulted in a positive impact, at least according to these testimonials.

It seems that there was a sense of relief that strong disagreements had not jeopardized the outcome of the Bible conference. In his diary, Clifton L. Taylor wrote at the beginning of the conference, the "big guns are firing broadsides with ammunition from Dan. 11." On another day, he noted that the "discussion waxed warm on Dan. 11." Despite these positive, public testimonials, one participant noted, at least privately, that there were strong feelings about various issues debated during the 1919 Bible Conference.[3]

Throughout the conference, there were a number of conversations about holding another Bible conference to continue what had begun at these meetings—perhaps the 1919 Conference would mark the beginning of such meetings annually. Yet it would be an entire generation before another major Bible conference would be held, in 1952. This may in part be due to the vitriolic attacks of Claude Holmes and J. S. Washburn, who perceived the 1919 meetings as the proof of Adventist apostasy.

Their attacks, through a series of pamphlets, contributed to the overthrow of A. G. Daniells as General Conference president in 1922 or, at the very least, Holmes and Washburn rejoiced at his loss of office. Daniells was not the only casualty. B. G. Wilkinson, the conservative president of Washington Missionary College, felt that E. F. Albertsworth was too liberal. As a result, a group of students testified against Albertsworth, citing his use of modernist textbooks. Albertsworth eventually left church employment as a consequence.[4]

Except for these public reports, coupled with attacks by a few detractors, the 1919 Bible Conference was largely forgotten over the next few years. That is, until they were accidentally discovered five decades later.

Discovery of the transcripts

In 1974, Donald Mansell, an employee of the Ellen G. White Estate, asked F. Donald Yost to look for any transcripts related to the 1919

Bible Conference in conjunction with research being conducted for the very first edition of the *Seventh-day Adventist Encyclopedia*. At the time, Yost had organized numerous boxes in the General Conference basement into an actual archive and served as its first director.

Several months later, in early 1975, Yost found a box of Conference transcripts and shared them with Mansell. As they read the candid discussions about Ellen G. White, the two quickly realized that they had stumbled on something very significant. They shared the transcripts with Arthur L. White, at the time secretary (director) of the White Estate. He deemed them significant enough to make copies to send to the White Estate research centers.[5]

Most Adventists learned about the transcripts when some of the most controversial excerpts from the dialogues about Ellen G. White, discussed in chapter 7, were printed in *Spectrum: Journal of the Association of Adventist Forums*—an independent Adventist magazine founded in 1970.[6] The publication of these excerpts was unsettling for many Adventists, some of whom reflected publicly, as well as in interviews, about how their publication was nothing short of an explosive event in the Adventist theological landscape of the 1970s. Such candid discussions about the nature of Inspiration and Ellen G. White's prophetic authority, taking place so soon after her death, were startling for many Adventist intellectuals.

The story of how these transcripts came to be published is interesting. Molleurus Couperus, a recently retired professor of the School of Medicine at Loma Linda University, learned about the transcripts from Mansell. On a research trip to the General Conference, Couperus, the founding editor of *Spectrum* from 1970 to 1976, studied the transcripts and made copies of them. Upon his return home, he edited them.

He contacted the editor, Roy Branson, who recommended their publication despite the fact that *Spectrum* did not have permission to do so. Branson did consult the journal's editorial board, which agreed to the transcripts' publication. In response to criticism, Couperus defended the decision to publish, stating that he had not signed any document limiting the use of the copies he had made. In retrospect, Branson said he believed that "this was the single most important issue" of *Spectrum* ever published. "People were stunned," he remarked, "that there were leaders of our church who tracked views similar to Adventist academics."[7]

Despite the initial controversy surrounding their publication, major studies of Adventist history quickly recognized the significance of this event. Afterward, every major treatment of Adventist history would at least mention the 1919 Bible Conference as a major turning point in Adventist history. Thus, the 1919 Bible Conference, although significant at the time it was held, did not become a major historic event in the church until after the discovery of the transcripts.

---

1. Report of Bible Conference, July 19, 1919, 1066, 1067, 1075. See also W. E. Howell, "Bible and History Teachers' Council," *Review and Herald*, August 14, 1919, 29; W. E. Howell, "Bible and History Teachers' Council," *Review and Herald*, September 25, 1919, 27, 28.

2. Report of Bible Conference, July 19, 1919, 1072.

3. Clifton L. Taylor diary, July 7, 8, 9, 1919.

4. Minutes of the Board of Trustees, Columbia Hall, February 20, 1919, 1, 2, February 10–15, 1920, 3, 4. For additional details, see Michael W. Campbell, "The 1919 Bible Conference and Its Significance for Seventh-day Adventist History and Theology" (PhD diss., Andrews University, 2008), 192, 193.

5. Donald Mansell, telephone interview by the author, September 27, 2006.

6. Molleurus Couperus, "The Bible Conference of 1919," *Spectrum: Journal of the Association of Adventist Forums* 10, no. 1 (May 1979): 23–57.

7. Roy Branson, telephone interview by the author, June 14, 2007.

Chapter 10

Legacy

The 1919 Bible Conference illustrates the danger of theological polarization. The real significance of this historic gathering is that it showcases the increasing polarization that was growing within Adventism and that came out clearly in the debates. The self-styled progressives and traditionalists were both much closer to each other than either group realized, but as they debated, they pushed each other farther apart.

One of my seminary professors would sometimes tell students that there should be an eleventh commandment in the Bible: "Thou shalt not do theology against thy neighbor." Although church leaders saw the importance of having candid discussions as a key to attaining theological unity, unfortunately, it appeared to have the opposite effect. There is no indication that the two camps continued to dialogue after the meeting. Instead, it would be another generation before church leaders would attempt another major Bible conference in 1952.

The 1919 Bible Conference also provides insight into a critical period in Seventh-day Adventist history—a time when the denomination was wrestling with the nature and authority of Ellen G. White's writings soon after her death in 1915. Issues surrounding the nature and authority of her writings arose in conjunction with debates about how to interpret Bible prophecy. The two hermeneutical camps articulated two different hermeneutical approaches to inspired writings, especially when it came to questions about how to interpret Ellen G. White's writings and their relationship to the Bible. These issues were not settled in 1919 but would continue to be a topic of debate through the rest of the twentieth century and even into our current century.

The 1919 Bible Conference reveals the pervasive influence of the emerging Fundamentalist Movement within Adventism. Both the progressives and traditionalists hailed the rising Prophecy Conference Movement and the publication of *The Fundamentals* as decisive events that Adventists should recognize and benefit from. Similarly, they all saw the rise of modernism as a grave threat, even though they embraced many modernist assumptions about how to view the world around them.

Historian Geoffrey Treloar suggests that during the late 1910s there was some fluidity among those conservative evangelicals who eventually became Fundamentalists.[1] All saw themselves within a common cause, but there was some variation. Many conservative evangelicals were more moderate and very closely resembled the progressives at the 1919 Bible Conference. Historically speaking, both groups present at the 1919 Bible Conference should be seen as variations of conservative, evangelical Christianity, aligned in common cause against modernism and similar threats. All Adventists recognized the importance of the divine Inspiration of the Bible.

Yet at the crux of the hermeneutical divide within the Seventh-day Adventist Church was the nature of this Inspiration. Fundamentalists were somewhat fluid at this early stage, even as some began to push for inerrancy. Similarly, within Adventism were some, such as A. T. Jones, who had pushed for an inerrant Ellen G. White. Veteran church leaders, although they saw that they had much in common with the rising Fundamentalist Movement, recognized there were problematic aspects involved in adopting a literalistic stance on inerrancy with regard to the Ellen G. White's writings. Yet as these leaders disappeared from the scene, the popularity of inerrancy gained increasing traction in Adventist literature during the 1920s. Still, there remained voices of moderation, and Adventism would continue to wrestle with the nature of Inspiration through the rest of the twentieth century.

Perhaps the great lesson of the 1919 Bible Conference showcases just how dangerous theological polarization can be within Adventism. The majority on both sides were far closer to each other than either side would like to admit. Yet, as they debated one another, they pushed each other farther apart. Thus, the 1919 Bible Conference highlights a hermeneutical divide in which for the first time in Adventist history, the progressives and the traditionalists waged war against one another about how to interpret Ellen G. White's writings. Although the individuals and issues would change, the same underlying hermeneutical divide would dominate all subsequent theological debates to the present. What was needed after the 1919 Bible Conference was more dialogue, not less. One can only imagine what might have been possible if instead of becoming polarized, participants at the 1919 Bible Conference had ventured to understand each other better and had continued to do so as a way of following up this epochal meeting.

If Adventists can learn from this conflict, it might just be possible to use these insights from the past to build constructive bridges of dialogue, understanding, and, possibly, even healing. After the 1919 conference, Adventism came perilously close to strange, almost alien, positions in its flirtation with the rising Fundamentalist movement. In reaction to that experience, some academics and intellectuals in the church began advocating in the 1970s for a new alliance with a neoorthodox style of liberalism. Of course, this caused some conservatives to retreat to the comforting, if intellectually and spiritually moribund, enclave of Fundamentalism. In this way, the same dynamic of polarization evident in 1919 continues to exist within Adventism today.

In order to survive and thrive, the Adventism of the future must find the balanced, thoughtful orthodoxy that Prescott, Daniells, and W. C. White were pointing toward during and after the 1919

Conference. Until that time, we will continue to live in the shadows of that defining event.

---

1. Geoffrey R. Treloar, *The Disruption of Evangelicalism: The Age of Torrey, Mott, McPherson, and Hammond* (Downers Grove, IL: InterVarsity Press, 2017), viii, 2, 14.

Top: The official photograph showing delegates to the 1919 Bible Conference standing in front of the newly constructed Columbia Hall. It was published in the *Review and Herald* along with official reports about the 1919 Bible Conference. This photograph showcases fifty-four participants. Church president A. G. Daniells (with the white goatee) is front and center.

Photograph courtesy of the Center for Adventist Research

Bottom: This second photograph of the editors at an editorial convention that took place shortly before the 1919 Bible Conference. This picture containing twenty-eight individuals showcases many of the same individuals who participated in both meetings. Two of the most prominent are W. W. Prescott (front row, far left with white shoes), and in the front and center, A. G. Daniells (again, sporting a white goatee). Notice that some of the delegates have placed their coats to the side due to the sweltering heat on the unfinished masonry work.

Photograph courtesy of the Ellen G. White Estate, Inc.

Top: The 1919 Bible Conference was held in the newly constructed Columbia Hall. This photograph, circa 1920s, shows what it looked like after construction was completed.

Bottom: Inside view of the Columbia Hall Chapel where the meetings for the 1919 Bible Conference took place.

Photographs courtesy of Weis Library at Washington Adventist University

Left: This photograph, circa 1920, shows General Conference president Arthur G. Daniells (1858–1935) close to the time of the 1919 Bible Conference. It was under his leadership that the denomination held this pivotal meeting, and he chaired many of the sessions.

Photograph courtesy of the Center for Adventist Research

Bottom: Photograph of Ellen G. White in casket. The death of Ellen G. White (1827–1915) left the Seventh-day Adventist Church without a living prophet. The legacy and authority of her writings, and how to properly interpret them, would eventually come to dominate the discussions at four pivotal points during the 1919 Bible Conference.

Photograph courtesy of the Ellen G. White Estate, Inc.

Right: One of the most visible personalities of the 1919 Bible Conference was William W. Prescott (1855–1943), veteran educator, editor, and administrator. During the conference he spoke more than any other single person, giving daily devotionals during the main Bible conference.

Left: Warren E. Howell (1869–1943) was the head of the Seventh-day Adventist Education Department. He chaired the planning committee and the sessions for the Bible and history teachers.

Left: Judson S. Washburn (1863–1955). He, along with Claude Holmes (1881–1953), pushed for an inerrant Ellen G. White that was equal to the Bible. They were vociferous in their opposition of A. G. Daniells and W. W. Prescott. As a consequence, they described the 1919 Bible Conference as a "diet of doubts."

Photograph courtesy of the Meredith family private collection

Right: Photograph of Benjamin G. Wilkinson (1872–1968), one of the leaders of the traditionalist (conservative) camp at the 1919 Bible Conference. Some handwritten notes indicate that Wilkinson borrowed copies of talks from the 1919 Bible Conference, possibly some of his own, from the 1919 Bible Conference transcripts, which appear to be no longer extant.

Left: Progressives at the 1919 Bible Conference who recognized problematic aspects of Inspiration, especially the inerrancy of Ellen G. White's writings, attributed the rise of this interpretative school of thought to Alonzo T. Jones (1850–1923) of 1888 fame. Jones took a very literalistic methodology and used her writings as a lens for interpreting the Bible.

Photograph courtesy of the Ellen G. White Estate, Inc.

Right: The legacy of Dr. John Harvey Kellogg (1852–1943), who departed from the Seventh-day Adventist Church in 1907, still loomed large as A. G. Daniells reflected during the 1919 Bible Conference about the power struggle between them. He felt that Ellen G. White's support at this crucial time was what made him especially appreciative of Ellen G. White's prophetic ministry.

Photograph courtesy of the Center for Adventist Research

Left: The Battle of the Churches (Pacific Press, 1924) was a book written by William G. Wirth, a religion teacher from the College of Medical Evangelists (now Loma Linda University) who participated in the 1919 Bible Conference. This graphic cover portrays a priest with a sledge hammer knocking away at the foundation of the church. Only two choices exist: modernism versus Fundamentalism.

Bottom: This graphic picture, found in Seventh-day Adventist publications during the early 1920s, depicts a large gulf between Christianity versus modernist theology. This graphic helped to more clearly identify the enemy for Adventists, which was clearly modernism.

Photograph courtesy of the author

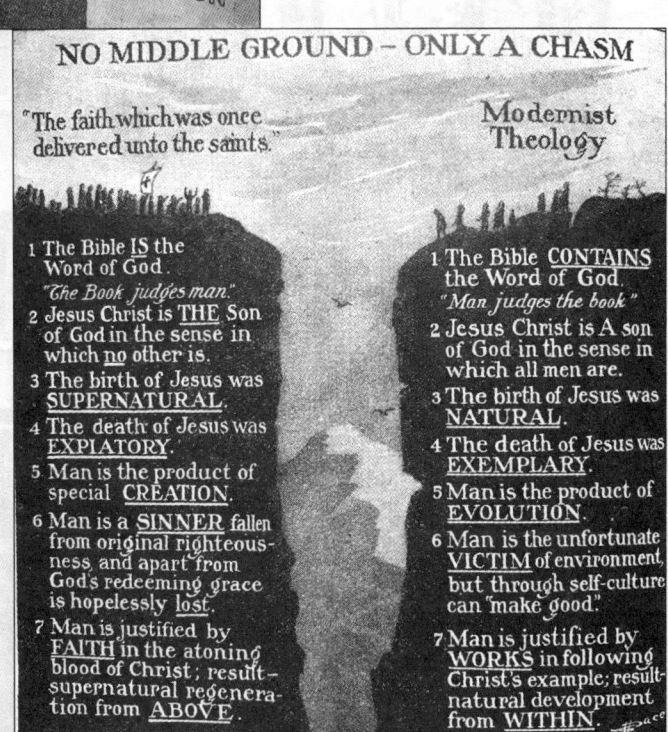

Left: Carlyle B. Haynes, a prominent Adventist minister during the 1920s and 1930s, wrote this book, *Christianity at the Crossroads* (Southern Publishing Association, 1924). The cover depicts a man at a crossroad between modernism and Fundamentalism—once again, only two choices exist for the Christian believer.

Bottom: This Adventist graphic depicts a Christian family taking refuge behind the Bible against the onslaught of a tidal wave of modernism. The depiction below states: "The rock-ribbed word of God withstands the tidal wave of Modernism that seems to sweep all before it."

Photograph courtesy of the author

The rock-ribbed word of God withstands the tidal wave of Modernism that seems to sweep all before it.